PANTAGES
THEATRE

REBIRTH OF A LANDMARK

PANTAGES
THEATRE

REBIRTH OF A LANDMARK

CONSTANCE OLSHESKI

Historical research by Mike Filey and John Lindsay

KEY PORTER BOOKS

**Canadian Cataloguing In
Publication Data**
Olsheski, Constance
Pantages Theatre
ISBN 1-55013-155-9
1. Pantages Theatre — History.
2. Theaters — Ontario — Toronto —
Conservation and restoration.
I. Filey, Mike. II. Title.
PN2306.T62P35 1989   792'.00713'541
C89-094087-8

Design: Ivan Holmes
Typesetting: Compeer Typographic
Services Ltd.
Printed and bound in Canada

Key Porter Books Limited
70 The Esplanade
Toronto, Ontario
Canada M5E 1R2

97 98 99 00 01 6 5 4 3 2

The author thanks Bramhall House for
permission to use material from *The
Best Remaining Seats*, by Ben M. Hall.

Frontispiece: The entrance lobby of
the Pantages theatre, restored to its
original splendour.

CONTENTS

FOREWORD

When the occasion presented itself to restore the site of Toronto's Pantages Theatre as a venue for live entertainment, we embraced it with a passion characteristic of our general approach to the entertainment business. We realized that we had been given a glorious opportunity to make an important contribution to the city's cultural life.

Although chiefly identified with motion pictures, we have endeavoured in recent years to make the most of any chance that came our way to bring great works of music and drama to audiences that would appreciate and enjoy them.

And although our operations reach cities and towns all over North America and Great Britain, we are proud to have Toronto as our home, and we are committed to strengthening our presence in this city.

To achieve a faithful restoration of the theatre required significant archival research of the theatre and the community which it served. That research, which retraced the community life from the mid-1800s to the 1930s, revealed Toronto's incredibly rich experience in all forms of entertainment. We could understand and appreciate why this city has constituted, for its size, the liveliest audience for drama, opera, vaudeville, music and of course, motion pictures on the entire North American continent.

From our first internal discussions of the project, we were determined that the resurrection of the Pantages would bring to today's theatre audiences the feelings of awe and enchantment that were engendered in audiences seventy years ago by the original elegant edifice. Not only that, we were resolved to create a theatre capable of accomodating technologically the best productions from all the world's stages, as well as the best works of our own Canadian artists and writers.

We were extremely fortunate to find that Toronto was rich in the human resources that were absolutely vital to the success of the

project — architects, engineers, artists, and craftsmen who not only had the necessary skills, but who shared our conviction that we were all involved in a labour of love to complete this massive restoration on time and on budget. I thank every one of them very sincerely for all they have done to make our dream a reality.

Garth H. Drabinsky

Special thanks to the sponsors of The Phantom of the Opera, who through their financial assistance, have helped to ensure that the Pantages story is told.

ACKNOWLEDGEMENTS

Pantages Theatre: Rebirth of a Landmark is the result of the efforts of many dedicated and talented people whose lives have all been affected by the theatre's restoration and resurrection.

Acknowledgement is graciously extended to the following people:

Garth H. Drabinsky for his vision, determination and inspiration to resurrect the theatre to its earlier glory and for his continued enthusiasm and dedication, without which the Pantages would not be;

Mike Filey for his research of the history of Toronto and for the full access to his photographic archives;

John Lindsay for his invaluable research and consultation;

Richard Roberts for his wisdom and for the eloquence he provided to the text;

Lynda Friendly for her comprehensive acquisition of archival photographs and her careful and meticulous review and editing of the story of the theatre's restoration;

David Mesbur and Peter Kofman for their guidance, direction and skills in executing the restoration project and for providing the insight on this project that could only have been acquired after spending over a year on the theatre's design and reconstruction;

Fiona Spalding-Smith for her superb photography which captured the breadth and splendour of the restoration project;

Joe and Ken Radford for their insight and recollection of their childhood days spent in the Pantages and for the use of cherished photographs of their father and the vaudeville stars who performed with the orchestra;

The Jackson-Lewis Company, Limited for use of the historical and original construction photographs of the Pantages; and

Ivan Holmes for his design of the book which evokes the true spirit of the theatre.

The auditorium of the Pantages
Theatre, completely restored to its
1920s splendour.

Opening night of the completely
restored Pantages Theatre, Wednesday,
September 20, 1989.

Almost seventy years after the curtain first rose at the Pantages, opening night guests marvel at the restored theatre's spectacular lobby.

TORONTO'S FINEST
THEATRE

Toronto had been a theatre town long before the opening of the Pantages in 1920. A hundred years earlier, stage plays were being presented in various makeshift theatrical settings. However, it wasn't until 1846 that Toronto's first real theatre was erected on the south side of King Street, midway between Bay and York streets, about where the main tower of the Toronto-Dominion Centre complex now stands. On January 12, 1846, the Royal Lyceum opened with a production of Sheridan's *The School for Scandal*, presented by the Toronto Amateur Theatrical Society. A short time later, a professional company from England, under the direction of a Mr. Skerett, took over the Royal Lyceum and put on a number of performances. Lack of interest on the part of the public soon caused the troupe's demise, which was recorded by a local theatre historian: "[Mr. Skerett's] expenses were far in advance of his receipts, and the season came to an abrupt close before the date first appointed. The fault was not his own, for he had brought a good dramatic company, in which was included his wife; but his efforts to provide a high class of dramatic entertainment were not sufficiently appreciated, and he left the city with an unfavourable impression of its inhabitants."

Early theatrical performances in Toronto were usually confined to fairly straightforward renditions of popular plays. As early as May 1847, however, the Royal Lyceum posted a playbill for a farce titled *'Twas I*. This may have been the city's first departure from the more serious dramas its theatres had been presenting, since it was the first playbill that intentionally offered something to make audiences laugh.

The theatre district grew slowly over the next thirty years. Although the population was growing rapidly, Toronto remained "The City of Churches," and most clergymen preached that the theatre was "the gateway to Hell." One important entertainment venue that did come into existence during this period was the St. Lawrence Hall at King and Jarvis streets. The hall frequently presented live performances, most often of the purely musical variety. In the late

A view of the stage of the Pantages, circa 1920, with its handpainted grand drape and private box seating.

The Royal Lyceum was one of Toronto's first live theatres. Erected in 1846 and located on the south side of King, between Bay and York streets, it presented dramatic productions. The Royal Lyceum was destroyed by fire in January, 1874.

The Crystal Palace was built in 1860 on King Street West and copied the style of its famous London, England, namesake. It was constructed of glass framed in iron and was moved to the grounds of the Canadian National Exhibition, where the building was used on occasions as a concert venue. Fire destroyed the Crystal Palace in 1906.

1850s and early 1860s, other buildings that were used for entertainment were added — the Crystal Palace on King Street West (later to be moved to the Exhibition Grounds to become the fair's first permanent building), the Horticultural Pavilion in Allan Gardens, the Yorkville Town Hall on Yonge Street north of Bloor, and the Music Hall in the Mechanics' Institute on Church Street (where the Toronto Public Library system was born in 1883).

In 1874, a new 1,750-seat theatre called the Grand Opera House was built near the southwest corner of Yonge and Adelaide streets. It opened on September 21, 1874, with a presentation of that old favourite, *The School for Scandal*, featuring an all-Canadian cast. Unfortunately, Toronto's taste for local talent proved ephemeral. The Canadian performers, at least in the principal roles, were soon replaced by touring stars from England and the United States.

The Grand Opera House was destroyed by fire in 1878 but was

$50,000 REWARD

Missing from his home in this city since
December 2nd, 1919

Ambrose J. Small

I am authorized by Mrs. Ambrose J. Small and Capital Trust Corporation to offer a reward of $50,000 for information leading to the discovery of the present whereabouts of the above named man, if alive.

Description: Age 53, 5ft. 6 or 7 ins.; 135 to 140 lbs. Blue eyes, sallow complexion. Brown hair and moustache, streaked with grey. Hair receding on temples. Is very quick in his movements.

Mr. Small, who is well known in theatrical circles in the United States and Canada, was owner of Grand Opera House, Toronto, and was last seen in his office at this theatre on afternoon of December 2nd, 1919.

When last seen he was wearing a dark tweed suit and dark overcoat with velvet collar and a soft felt hat.

The above photo, although taken some time ago is a good likeness, except that for a considerable time previous to his disappearance he had been wearing his moustache clipped short.

I am also authorized to offer in the alternative, a reward of $15,000 for information leading to the discovery of the present whereabouts of the body of the above named man, if dead.

The information must be received before September 1st, 1920, on which date the above offers of rewards will expire.

All previous offers of rewards are withdrawn.

Wire all information to the undersigned.

H. J. GRASETT,
Chief Constable.

POLICE HEADQUARTERS.
TORONTO
June 1st. 1920.

rebuilt soon afterwards. For a time, it was owned by Ambrose Small, whose disappearance in 1919, along with $1 million in cash after the sale of his theatrical empire for $2 million, provided the city with an unsolved mystery that has become a Toronto legend.

Live theatre flourished in the 1870s and 1880s with no less than ten theatres opening — and sometimes closing. Several had been converted from such diverse previous uses as a roller skating rink, a Yonge Street had become the theatre district by 1874. In that year, the Grand Opera House was constructed on the south side of Adelaide between Yonge and Bay streets. The 1,750-seat theatre was demolished in 1927 because of the declining interest in opera.

produce market, and even the city's first zoological gardens, situated where the Royal York Hotel now stands. These theatres offered a wide variety of theatrical productions, ranging from *The Hunchback*, described in the local papers as a "beautiful five-act play," to the Royal Opera House presentation of the first Canadian performance of Gilbert and Sullivan's *H.M.S. Pinafore*. The latter was billed as "complete with forty people on the stage" who were to perform "the greatest musical success of the day" in "correct and elegant costumes."

In the fall of 1893, invited guests and curious passers-by gathered at the corner of Victoria and Shuter streets to watch and applaud as a young Charles Vincent Massey (who in 1952 would become Canada's first native-born Governor General) helped his grandfather to lay the cornerstone of what was to become one of the city's most active social centres. First known as the Massey Music Hall, this now venerable structure has seen almost every form of entertainment and public gathering, including opera, demonstrations against the vaccination of children, and the first moving pictures of the South African War. It was erected at a cost of $152,390.75 by Toronto industrialist Hart Massey, a stickler for precise accounting. He built it in memory of his son Charles Albert, who had died at the age of thirty-five of typhoid fever. Charles Albert had loved music, and his father thought it only fitting that a music hall be his memorial.

If the census people in Toronto in the year 1900 could have found another 957 people to enumerate, the city's population would have

Massey Hall was erected in memory of Charles Albert Massey by his father, Hart Massey.

Massey Hall, built in 1894, was the home of the Toronto Conservatory Orchestra, which later became the Toronto Symphony.

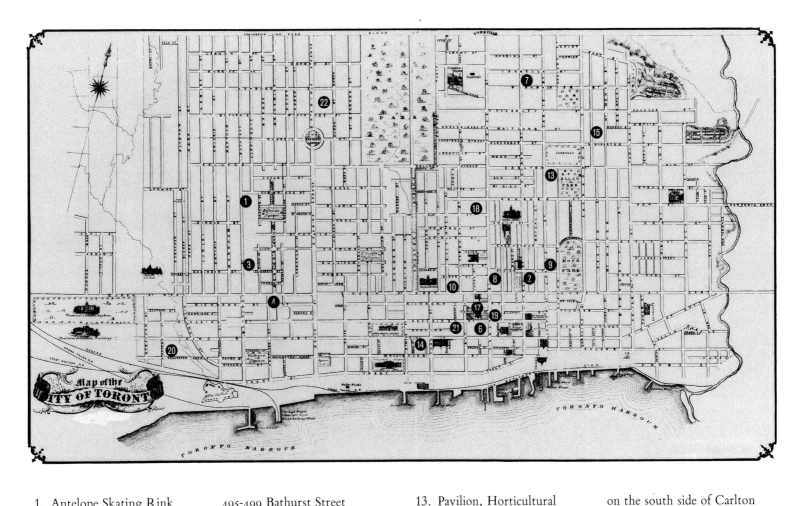

1. Antelope Skating Rink   495-499 Bathurst Street
2. Caledonian Skating Rink   78 Mutual Street
3. Elmdale Skating Rink   239 Bathurst Street
4. Grand Central Skating Rink   423 Queen Street West

*5. Grand National Rink   153 Brook Avenue
6. Grand Opera House   11 Adelaide Street West
7. Granite Curling and Skating Club   519 Church Street

8. Massey Music Hall   corner of Shuter Street and Victoria Street
9. Moss Park Rink   123 Shuter Street
10. New Bijou Theatre   26 Queen Street West
*11. Old Orchard Skating Rink   148 Harrison Avenue
*12. Parkdale Curling Rink   on the west side Cowan Avenue near Queen Street West

13. Pavilion, Horticultural Gardens   on the south side of Carlton Street between Jarvis Street and Sherbourne Street
14. Princess Theatre   167 King Street West
15. Prospect Park Skating Rink   south side Prospect Street at the corner of Ontario Street
*16. Queen City Rink   Queen Street West opposite Beaconsfield Avenue
17. Royal Theatre   22 Temperance Street
18. St. George's Rink   between 22-30 Elm Street
19. Shea's Theatre   91 Yonge Street
20. Stanley Park Rink   Wellington Avenue at the corner of Walnut Street
21. Toronto Opera House   25 Adelaide Street West
22. Victoria Skating Rink   259 Huron Street

*Not shown on map

The program cover for the two-week-long activities of the 1892 Industrial Fair in Toronto.

reached the impressive figure of 200,000. As it was, the 199,043 Toron-tonians who *were* counted certainly had a wealth of things to do and places to go. The Toronto city directory of 1901 records under "Amusement, Places of" four theatres, two opera houses, one music hall, two curling rinks, one horticultural pavillion and twelve skating rinks. Apart from the fact that Torontonians must have spent a lot of time ice skating, the directory reveals the emergence of vaudeville in Toronto. A new 2,000-seat entertainment palace, called the Shea's Theatre, had opened two years earlier. Several other vaudeville the-atres, including a second built by Jerry Shea at Richmond and Victoria streets, sprang up in the next twenty years, as well as a few burlesque houses. Live theatre, however, was still king. The Grand Opera House was flourishing and so was the Princess. These were joined in 1907 by the Royal Alexandra on King Street West.

Paralleling this activity in live theatre was the development of motion pictures. These were first projected onto a blank wall at Koster and Bial's Music Hall in New York City on April 23, 1896. Four months later, a Buffalo entrepreneur opened Robinson's Musee on Toronto's lower Yonge Street with an "epic" entitled *The Kiss*, star-ring John C. Rice and Whitby, Ontario's own Mae Irwin. Toron-

At the turn of the century, ice skating and hockey were as popular outdoors as live theatre was indoors. In 1900, Toronto boasted thirteen skating rinks, which were enjoyed by men and women alike.

tonians flocked to the new movie house to pay the ten-cent admission fee and sit spellbound while a hand-cranked Edison Vitascope projected dancing images onto a painted screen. The film ran through the projector once and was collected in a clothes basket to be rerun for the next audience.

That same year, at the Toronto Industrial Exhibition (later renamed the Canadian National Exhibition), the Lumière Cinématographe, a somewhat similar projection device imported from France, was introduced. It too became an instant success with such films as *Coronation of the Czar*, *The Derby and Everything About It*, and *The Henley Regatta*. After the Exhibition was over, its general manager, H.J. Hill, rented a store opposite Robinson's Musee and started to show the same sort of programming. Originally planned to last ten days, popular demand kept Hill's rather primitive entertainment package going for ten weeks, after which he took it on tour to large and

Architect John Lyle designed the Royal Alexandra in a French Renaissance style. The impressive theatre was built in 1907 and offered Torontonians popular musical comedies.

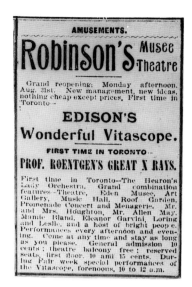

An advertisement for Toronto's first theatre to show moving pictures or vitascope performances, as they were then called. Its audience was less affluent than those of the live theatre venues and the musee offered this new form of entertainment for ten cents.

small communities all over the province. By charging twenty-five cents and playing in YMCAs, Masonic Temples, and public libraries, Hill was able to turn a tidy profit. In many towns, the movies stole audiences from the music halls and playhouses. The handwriting was on the wall.

Toronto's first permanent motion picture theatre opened in 1906 on the east side of Yonge Street, just north of Queen. Toronto-born John Griffin, a travelling circus performer, had often visited the new motion picture houses that were springing up everywhere in the United States. Returning home in the late winter of 1906, Griffin rented a recently vacated jewellery store directly opposite Timothy Eaton's busy emporium. He gutted the store, painted a white square on one wall, bought and set up a projector, installed a hundred or so rented kitchen chairs in nice, even rows, and in March began to show all-film programs in his Theatorium.

At the same time, two brothers, Jule and Jay J. Allen, were doing something similar in Brantford, Ontario. Not content with one location, however, they slowly expanded their business into a chain of more than fifty picture palaces from coast to coast. In Toronto alone, there were seven large Allen picture houses and another three smaller ones by 1920.

One of the more than fifty motion picture theatres owned by the Allen brothers, Canada's first owners of a national theatre circuit.

NATHAN NATHANSON'S DREAM

Another Canadian chain was begun in 1916 by thirty-year-old Nathan Louis Nathanson. Financed by billboard king E.L. Ruddy, its first purchase was the Majestic Theatre, a dingy and disreputable vaudeville house on Adelaide Street, near Yonge, which had been formerly owned by Ambrose Small. After months of extensive and expensive renovations, the Majestic was transformed into an elegant 1,175-seat motion picture house and renamed the Regent. Shortly thereafter, Nathanson bought the Strand on lower Yonge Street (on the site of Robinson's Musee) and constructed the Alhambra on Bloor Street, just west of

Located on the north side of Bloor Street, just west of Bathurst, the Alhambra was the first theatre to be built by Nathanson exclusively for the presentation of moving pictures or photoplays as they were also called. In order to compete with vaudeville, which was at its height, photoplay houses presented music with the silent films they showed. The Alhambra, later renamed the Eve, was demolished in 1989.

Nathan Louis Nathanson, founder of Famous Players Canadian Corporation, was Canada's entertainment mogul from 1915 to 1929. His vision of building the largest and best theatre circuit in the country led to the construction of the Pantages theatre.

Bathurst. By 1920 Nathanson's chain had expanded to twenty theatres that interested Adolph Zukor, Hollywood mogul and president of Famous Players-Lasky Corp. Together they formed Famous Players Canadian Corp. In 1922, when the Allen brothers ran into financial difficulties, Famous Players added this chain to its own, thereby becoming Canada's largest.

Even before that, however, in 1919, Nathanson had decided to build Canada's largest vaudeville house in the heart of downtown Toronto. He was well aware of the city's reputation as "The Greatest Showtown in Canada." He also knew that building and operating such a theatre would provide the impetus he needed to make his dream of heading the country's largest theatrical circuit a reality.

He set out to augment his existing group with the combination of financiers, architects, and program-booking agents necessary to

To finance the $1-million construction of the Pantages, its owners, Eastern Theatres Limited, made a public offering of shares. In 1919, this advertisement in *The Evening Telegram* provided potential shareholders with information on the new theatre.

fulfil his vision. On the financial side, he drew together a group that included J.P. Bickell, president of McIntyre Porcupine Mines, J.B. Tudhope, of Tudhope automobile fame, and W.D. Ross, who later was appointed Lieutenant-Governor of Ontario. Together they formed Eastern Theatres Limited, with the object of raising $1 million by means of public stock issue.

The architect was an obvious choice. Not only was Thomas Lamb one of the world's best known and most prolific theatre architects, but his work also spanned every type of theatre design. His career began in the days of the nickelodeon and reached its height during the golden age of the vaudeville and movie palaces. In the fifteen years

Catherine Duggan was one of the first shareholders in the Pantages. This is the stock certificate she received in 1922.

27

from 1910 to 1925, his specialty was the vaudeville theatre.

The last major issue for Nathanson to settle concerned the type of programming that would attract audiences to his theatre. The timing proved fortunate for both Nathanson and the vaudeville circuit operator of his choice, Alexander Pantages. Pantages was the sole owner of the most important independent vaudeville theatre chain in North America and could therefore offer top quality performers to star in productions at Nathanson's new theatre. Up to 1919, however, the Pantages chain had been concentrated almost exclusively on the West Coast because the tightly controlled eastern market was dominated by kingpins Benjamin Keith, Ed Albee, and Marcus Loew in New York, and by the Orpheum Circuit in Chicago. Pantages, who already operated several theatres in western Canada, was eager to expand in the east. He seized upon the opportunity to have his name associated with Canada's newest and largest vaudeville palace.

Pantages was a self-made multi-millionaire, who had led an incredible life. Born into poverty in Greece in 1871, he escaped a bleak future by stowing away on a ship to South America when he was only seven years old. He spent the rest of his pre-adolescence working on ships that took him all over the world. His teenage years were spent as a construction worker in the jungles of Panama, where he worked on France's abortive effort to construct the Panama Canal. The deplorable working conditions and his frequent bouts of malaria made him later look back on these years as the most difficult of his life. He finally escaped by signing on as a member of the crew of a brigantine sailing for Puget Sound, Washington. From Seattle he made his way to San Francisco, where he kept himself alive by working as a shoeshine boy, then a waiter, and finally a prizefighter, although he seems to have had only one professional fight.

In 1897 at the age of twenty-six, Pantages joined the Klondike Gold Rush. After gambling away his entire stake of $1,000, he took a job as a waiter and became involved with a former Coney Island chorus girl named Kate Rockwell. Known as "Klondike Kate" and "The Belle of the Yukon," she was earning thousands of dollars a month in Dawson by singing and dancing for the sourdoughs. Pantages soon persuaded her to invest some of her money in a theatre that he and a group of friends wanted to open. Although Pantages knew little about the theatre business, under his management, the Orpheum in Dawson became a popular amusement hall. He himself swept up every night after closing, not because he was trying to give the impression that he was a hard worker, but for the very practical reason that he had observed many drunken miners accidently spilling gold dust on the floor.

Born into poverty in Greece in 1871, Alexander Pantages left his homeland at the age of seven and eventually worked his way to America. The self-made millionaire lived a life filled with excitement and controversy. His theatres were located on the west coast of the United States and Canada, with Toronto being the most easterly situated of the chain that bore his name.

After the gold rush was over, Pantages returned to Seattle, where he bought a combination shoeshine parlour and fruit stand next door to a theatre that was part of the Considine Vaudeville Circuit. The theatre was prospering as was the circuit to which it belonged. (Eventually, through various mergers and acquisitions, it would become the enormous Loew's Circuit.) Never one to miss an opportunity, Pantages set up his own vaudeville theatre, the first Pantages theatre, right across the street from the Considine. Using various dubious manoeuvres, he lured acts away from his competition and by 1909 he too had a chain of vaudeville houses on the West Coast. After building or leasing theatres in every important city in the northwest, his chain extended from Vancouver to Los Angeles and as far east as Kansas City. Pantages claimed that he was no real judge of talent but that he listened carefully to his audiences in order to be able to please their tastes. He must have succeeded in doing so because it was widely thought that no theatre of his ever lost money.

THE VAUDEVILLE/MOVIE PALACE

Show business in Toronto in 1920 was very competitive for a city of 500,000 people. Shea's Hippodrome, built in 1914 with more than 3,000 seats, was the Toronto home of the Keith and Orpheum circuits, and Loew's Uptown and Loew's Yonge Street (the latter with its upstairs Winter Garden) were booked by Loew's. The Princess was linked to the Shuberts, an American theatre circuit with important vaudeville connections, and the stately Royal Alexandra, although independent, was important enough to pick and choose from a variety of circuits. Two opera houses filled out the city's live entertainment scene.

Theatre owners were full of optimism in 1920. The boom times following World War I had made the future of vaudeville seem bright. The bill of fare provided by vaudeville/movie palaces was proving to be enormously successful. A theatre like New York's 5,000-seat Capitol presented six shows daily and could have a potential box office of up to 30,000 paying customers in one day! It could make a massive profit while charging the customers relatively little. Indeed, the Capitol was so successful that it influenced the thinking of many theatre owners, including Nathan Nathanson. It isn't surprising, therefore, that the Pantages and the Capitol had a great deal in common. Although the Capitol had 1,400 more seats than the Pantages (which had 3,600), both were the largest theatres in their respective countries. And both were designed by Thomas Lamb in the lavish style of the period.

Lamb and other architects, prompted by America's movie moguls, brought Hollywood to every main street in North America. The Capitol, Pantages, and other vaudeville/movie palaces that they created perfectly reflected their time; everything about them was extravagant and overpowering. Just as no stage show in the twenties could use too many stage effects or be too elaborate, so too could a theatre never have too much in the way of gilt, lacquer, cut glass, mirrors, broadloom, marble (real and otherwise), statuary, or chandeliers.

The vaudeville/movie palace was an opportunity for an architect to transport people from their ordinary houses or boring apartments to somewhere exotic and palatial. The surroundings in which the audience saw the show were an integral part of the whole experience. Well-known theatre architects and the most successful theatre owners had long been aware of this, and this awareness had nurtured the building boom of the grand palaces. In Ben Hall's book *The Golden Age of the Movie Palace*, one of Lamb's contemporaries summed up the rationale behind the grandeur of the movie palaces:

In 1929, $3.30 bought two tickets to a live performance at the Princess Theatre.

The auditorium and stage of the
Loew's Uptown on Yonge Street.
This vaudeville theatre was also
designed by Thomas Lamb and
contained many of the Adam and
Empire details found in the Pantages.

Watch the eyes of a child as it enters the portals of our great theatres and treads the pathway into fairyland. Watch the bright light in the eyes of the tired shopgirl who hurries noiselessly over carpets and sighs with satisfaction as she walks amid furnishings that once delighted the hearts of queens. See the toil-worn father whose dreams have never come true, and look inside his heart as he finds strength and rest within the theatre. There you have the answer to why motion picture theatres are so palatial.

Here is a shrine to democracy where there are no privileged patrons. The wealthy rub elbows with the poor—and are better for the contact. . . . These are not impractical attempts at showing off. These are part of a celestial city—a cavern of many-colored jewels, where iridescent lights and luxurious fittings heighten the expectation of pleasure. It is richness unabashed, but richness with a reason.

There were two schools of theatre design from which the great vaudeville/movie palaces were imagined and created. The "atmospheric" style, by using projected clouds and stars on the ceiling of the auditorium, or by simulating an outdoor garden, gave the audience the illusion of watching the show from the splendour of a palace courtyard. All theatres that were not atmospheric in style were known as standard or "hard top" theatres, and characteristically tried to imitate, or even outdo, elaborate theatres like the Paris Opera. Toronto's historic Runnymede and the Winter Garden are examples of the atmospheric style. New York's Capitol and Toronto's Pantages were hard tops.

The "movie palace" was not necessarily distinct from the "vaudeville theatre" from which it evolved. Some of the great movie palaces began their days as vaudeville theatres. Once the all-important theatre organ was added, they became movie palaces. Although only the large cities could claim genuine palaces with 2,000 or 3,000 or even more seats, some smaller centres had theatres whose opulence overshadowed their size. The Pantages, Lamb's Toronto masterpiece, had both size and opulence.

Thomas Lamb, born in Dundee, Scotland, in 1887, emigrated to the United States when he was twelve years old. He first came to prominence in 1909 when he was asked to design the City Theatre in New York. In a mere decade he became the pre-eminent theatre architect in the world. New York's famous Madison Square Garden was his and, amazingly, so were more than three hundred theatres in dozens of countries throughout the world. Although by 1919 Lamb realized that movies were being shown with increasing frequency in vaudeville houses, he was not yet designing his theatres as large movie palaces. His earlier (1913) Toronto effort, the combined Loew's and Winter Garden Theatres, consisted of two smaller auditoriums equipped with gas lighting because electricity was not always reliable in the early 1900s. The unique concept of building one auditorium above the other was the way in which Lamb made it possible to squeeze twice as many people into the same building without having to equip the audience with some kind of hearing assistance. Public address systems using stage microphones were not yet practical. But the combined theatres were never designed as places to show motion pictures. They later worked well as movie theatres due to the fact that a good theatre, with excellent sight lines and acoustics, is a good theatre whether it is used for drama, variety shows, or movies.

Lamb visualized the Toronto Pantages as the classic vaudeville theatre. Although during his extensive career he had designed both atmospheric and hard-top theatres, he favoured the latter. Having selected the hard-top model for the Pantages, he then designed the theatre in his favourite style of that period, which was based on the architecture of Robert Adam. Robert Adam (1728-1792) was one of four brothers, all of whom entered the architectural profession in the footsteps of their father, William Adam, one of the leading Scottish architects of his time. The Adam style was revived and copied by many architects in the nineteenth century and was particularly popular in Britain, where it was dubbed the Adam and Empire style. It continued to be popular at the beginning of the twentieth century.

The Adam style of architecture is a combination of a number of styles. Robert Adam was greatly stirred by two events—the rediscovery of Greek art as the original source of classic style, and the excavations at Herculaneum and Pompeii. These archaeological finds inspired Adam to create a new style of interior decor, adapted primarily from Roman stucco ornamentation. This style combined the delicacy of rococo interiors with a strongly neoclassic emphasis on plane surfaces, symmetry, and geometric precision. His walls and ceilings were decorated with mouldings of delicate oval fans and garlands, and were pierced with numerous panels and niches.

The Adam style has often been criticized as being merely a kind of decoration rather than architecture. Robert Adam's severest critics claimed that the over-elaborate plasterwork was similar to the efforts of a clever pastry chef, rather like the frosting on a wedding cake.

Remarkably similar criticisms were later to be heard of Thomas Lamb's theatre interiors in the twentieth century. Lamb's famous Adam and Empire style used fluted columns, damask hangings, arched organ grills over theatre boxes, and enormous domes. The usual plasterwork included fans and garlands in great abundance. These features had worked very well for him in his New York Capitol Theatre, and so he used them in the Pantages, as well as in many other theatres to

Renowned theatre architect, Thomas Lamb.

follow. According to Ben Hall in *The Golden Age of the Movie Palace*: "Lamb defended his unswerving allegiance to the Adam brothers on the grounds that he felt this style of decoration reflected the mood and preference of the American people." Despite the criticisms, Lamb became the most renowned theatre architect in history. In 1920, of the five vaudeville houses in Toronto, three had been designed by him: the Loew's Winter Garden with a combined seating capacity of over 3,000, the Loew's Uptown with a seating capacity of 3,000, and the Pantages.

With 3,600 seats, the Pantages ranked second in size to New York's Capitol, the world's largest and most elaborate vaudeville palace. But it was the Capitol's equal in grandeur! It was built on a residential site

The entrance and lobby of the Pantages, known as the Yonge Street link, circa 1920.

on Victoria Street, immediately east of the heart of Toronto's shopping district, because the price of property on Victoria was lower than that of busy Yonge Street. Nathanson did, however, purchase a narrow piece of property on Yonge Street to give the theatre an entrance on Toronto's main street.

What this entry hall lacked in width was certainly made up for in splendour. Over the elaborate box office was a curved pressed-metal and glass canopy lit by modern "electric lights." The striking key-shaped marquee above the canopy featured white tracer lights, red neon, and an antique bronze finish. After passing the box office, patrons entered a spacious grand hall measuring twenty-two feet wide by one

The upper lobby of the Pantages when it was first constructed in 1920.

hundred and twenty feet long. Its elaborate design featured bevelled-glass mirrors, Ionic columns, faux marble, and rich blue and gold draperies. Handpainted scenic murals by an artist named H. Farnsworth decorated each side of the lobby. Overhead was a high cross-vaulted ceiling hung with magnificent crystal chandeliers. Matching wall sconces accented the side walls.

This lobby led patrons from Yonge Street to the main building on Victoria Street, passing up and over a service lane between those two streets. At the end of the passageway, a flight of marble steps took theatregoers up to a set of etched glass doors, which opened onto the upper level of the two-storey grand lobby. As the whole audience rarely gathered at one time on this level, it served as a focal point from which the patrons could either enter the balcony or descend a split staircase directly into the orchestra level of the auditorium. The staircase was strikingly finished in fine imported marble. The bannister, which encircled the entire lobby, was crafted in a faux marble plaster technique known as "scagliola." On the wide stair landing was a backlit stained-glass arched panel, set into an illuminated aquarium. Over the landing, an impressive twenty-foot-long by seven-foot-high painted mural featured classical figures and motifs in a garden setting. The entire lobby was capped by a silver-leafed oval dome embellished with plaster ornamentation, circular medallions, and an elegant crystal chandelier.

The theatre auditorium itself fulfilled the promise suggested by the entrance passageway and lobby, as it was, to say the least, opulent. Although large, measuring 22,500 square feet, the auditorium did not appear cold or cavernous because of the careful attention to the choice and blend of colours. The walls were panelled in jacquard-woven fabric in deep blue, accented by gold threads against a predominantly gold-toned background.

A 1919 photograph of the original framing for the dome and the proud workmen who constructed it. The various plaster components of the dome are supported on black iron straps secured to the structural steel roof trusses above. The extensive attic space was utilized for ductwork as well as the organ loft.

The 3,600-seat auditorium of the
Pantages, circa 1920. The grand
staircase and its stained glass window
can be seen at the centre rear of the
orchestra level of the auditorium.

On each side of the auditorium were six sumptuous upper and lower private boxes entered through rich blue- and gold-draped archways. The faces of the boxes, as well as the front of the balcony, were finished in elaborately carved and decorated plasterwork. Over the boxes, the pipe organ was concealed behind gilded arched organ screens. An additional echo organ was located in the space above the main ceiling near the rear of the auditorium.

The great width of the auditorium allowed for a wide and high proscenium arch. Elaborately carved in decorative plaster, and completely finished in gold leaf, it framed a large stage. The sheer size of the one hundred-foot-wide auditorium was impressive, while the width of the stage, between the proscenium arches, was fifty feet, and its height thirty-six feet. There was nearly seventy feet of wing space. These dimensions far exceeded those of most other theatres, not only in 1920, but today as well.

The magnificent velvet house curtain, with its pelmet of swag drapes, was a beautiful shade of deep blue, hung with gold rope. The travelling hand-painted grand drape behind it was designed by a young Russian artist, John Wenger, who was inspired, so it was said, by Maeterlinck's *Bluebird*. This curtain was reputed to be a replica of one in New York's Capitol Theatre. The curved soundboard above the proscenium featured a three-panel painted mural, again depicting classical figures in the style of the lobby paintings.

Thomas Lamb achieved at the Pantages one of his most architecturally unified compositions, through the careful integration of line, curve, and detail. The entire auditorium was decorated with hundreds

By the beginning of December, 1919, excavation and foundation work for the Pantages was well advanced. It was important to complete as much of the underground work as possible before the ground froze.

The Victoria Street entrance provided
access for the few patrons who arrived
by car, in the 1920s.

of connecting plaster mouldings in an astonishing array of designs and motifs. Most of these were executed by J.J. Haines, "Plaster Artist Extraordinaire." Even the crowning glory of the auditorium, the elegant circular ceiling dome, finished in deep green and gold, was linked with the side wall boxes and proscenium by sweeping curved cornices and decorative mouldings.

Not all of the design effort was spent on decorative effects, as patron comfort and convenience were also considered. Sight lines and acoustics were excellent, and the theatre provided for smoking lounges and "retiring rooms" on both lobby levels. *Construction Magazine*, in its review of the Pantages in November, 1920, titled it "the pioneer of large theatres in Toronto." It noted that the Victoria Street entrance was "provided primarily for the accommodation of motorists," surely a unique and innovative idea at the time. In addition, the magazine noted that "special care has been given to the ventilating apparatus, the fresh air being brought in from the outside, washed and tempered, and forced through ducts in the auditorium and then expelled through vents in the ceiling."

The Pantages Theatre was reported to have cost between $600,000 and $1,000,000 to build, making it Toronto's costliest. The general contractor was Jackson-Lewis Co. Limited of Toronto, which is still in business today. Despite the theatre's size and beauty, it was built in less than a year, partly because many of its decorative elements were prefabricated in one of the professional decorating studios in New York from which many of Lamb's mouldings originated. These delicate and intricate details were then installed in the appropriate locations. Even the great oval balustrade in the grand lobby was prefabricated and installed in this way.

In 1920, male patrons were provided with this elegant smoking lounge.

Other aspects of the construction proved to be more of a challenge. The proscenium over Canada's largest stage was supported by a concrete girder twelve feet deep by two feet, two inches wide, with a clear span of fifty-one feet. Each end was supported on a six-foot, ten-inch by two-foot, two-inch solid masonry pier. The *Contract Record*, in an article on December 22, 1920, described the difficulty of installing one of the largest girders ever poured in Toronto at that time: "The pouring was continuous and took fourteen labourers and two engineers twelve hours to complete. It took place in December during cold weather and, to protect the concrete from frost, two one-inch steam pipes were run from end to end, one being placed three feet from the bottom of the girder and the other eight feet. After the concrete had set, these pipes were cut off and left in the girder." Despite the difficulty of forming and shoring the girder twenty-eight feet above the stage floor, when the forms were removed, it was found that the girder was only nine-sixteenths of an inch out of line.

The architecture and construction of the Pantages did not necessarily impress the artistic elite of the time. One critic was reported by the aforementioned Ben Hall to have strongly rejected the eclectic mixture of styles and decorative elements: "This irresponsible reproduction of all the great architectural treasures of the ages, so cheapen public taste that one wonders if a whole generation is not now arising whose artistic appreciation will be warped for years to come." The Pantages, however, was not built to gain approval from architectural purists. It was built for Toronto's avid theatregoers, who arrived by streetcar and paid forty-five cents admission. When they walked up the long lobby and climbed the marble staircase, they entered a fantasyland that allowed them to escape the drudgery and boredom of their world outside. For those few special hours in the Pantages, life would be merry, delightful and splendid, and their fantasy would be complete.

During the 1920s the key-shaped Pantages sign dominated the Yonge Street theatre area.

VAUDEVILLE AT THE PANTAGES

The Toronto Pantages opened its doors to an eager public on August 28, 1920. At that time, North America already had approximately 4,000 places of entertainment where vaudeville acts were performed. In Toronto alone there were several, notably Shea's Hippodrome, the Princess, Loew's Uptown and the combined Loew's Downtown and Elgin Winter Garden. Theatre owners were responding to the popularity of this rather new and varied form of entertainment by building theatres that had seating capacities averaging 1,500 seats. The demand was so high and insatiable that up to five or six performances a day were given, allowing a theatre to attract up to 9,000 patrons a day.

For the fifty years between 1875 to 1925, vaudeville reigned as the single most popular form of entertainment in North America. By the latter part of the nineteenth century, it had evolved into a series of unrelated acts, which might have included dancers, singers, animal acts, acrobats, jugglers, and other circus performers, all following one another in rapid succession. This sort of entertainment had existed in many countries for centuries. The art of mimicry and animal acts with elephants, lions, monkeys, and all the other animals now popularly associated with circuses, were popular in ancient Rome. The entertainers of ancient Egypt had mastered the art of magic, and singing minstrels were popular in Greece. Vaudeville in North America was a combination of all these art forms.

The word *vaudeville* had its origin in France in the fifteenth century. Credited with its creation was composer Olivier Basselin, who lived in the small community of Vau-de-Vire, literally "valley of the (river) Vire" in Normandy. Basselin's compositions, and those of his fellow artists, were both topical and satirical, and became known locally as the songs of Vau-de-Vire. Eventually some of these songs reached the theatres of Paris and by the eighteenth century they were being inserted into many of the farces then appearing on the Parisian stage. It wasn't long before their place of origin was corrupted to Vau-de-Ville or "valley of the city." The stage plays that contained

Tom Ellis and Viola West, two of the many Canadian performers that graced the Pantages' stage, performed at the Pantages in July, 1928.

these satirical snippets were then referred to as "comédies avec vaudeville," a description that has been simplified to the present term *vaudeville*. The name spread all over the world, and a patron of a vaudeville house, wherever it might be, would expect to find uplifting entertainment that would build, act by act, in excitement and amusement.

There were no vaudeville theatres in Britain, not because the British did not enjoy such high-spirited entertainment, but because the government deliberately prohibited the construction of such theatres so as to reduce the competition for the established legitimate houses. Theatres presenting live performances were regulated by a royal licence that permitted drama but not music and dancing. Patrons were allowed to drink beer and to smoke, which led to a much rowdier atmosphere in British theatres than theatres in North America. Although these rules were later changed, and music and dancing were permitted, Britain never came to refer to its equivalent entertainment venues as vaudeville theatres but instead called them variety theatres or music halls.

The North American tradition of vaudeville had a considerably more refined beginning than that of the British, especially in the days prior to World War I, when it was usually advertised as "family entertainment." One of the first recorded uses of the word *vaudeville* on the west side of the Atlantic is found in the name of a theatre company of 1871 — "Sargent's Great Vaudeville Company." Back in those days, in addition to stage plays, audiences were entertained by "buskers," who charged no admission but passed a hat after their performances; minstrels, the successors of wandering minstrels; min-

A 1918 view of Yonge Street, looking north to the future site of the Pantages from the Loew's vaudeville theatre.

strel shows in blackface; and burlesque shows. By 1875, however, family-oriented vaudeville had become predominant in most parts of North America. Although in some instances "strippers" did go on the vaudeville stage, their performances were less risqué than in the burlesque houses. For all we know, "Salome," in her Dance of the Seven Veils at the Pantages, may have dropped all seven, but there were still some rather strategic garments left.

North American vaudeville was a unique form of entertainment, since it achieved a warmth and closeness with the audience that its counterpart, legitimate theatre, did not. An act was often well rehearsed, particularly if it had toured across the continent, but it still had freshness and spontaneity because the performers modified their act to suit the audience in front of them. Charles and Louise Samuels in their book *Once Upon a Stage, The Merry World of Vaudeville*, describe the vaudeville experience:

It was the pleasure and pride [of the vaudeville artists] to project warmth, laughter, and elation. And what they gave out across the footlights worked like magic. To the folks out front it was as though they too had triumphed over their troubles and sorrows and were up there singing like angels, dancing like wizards, cracking jokes that lifted the roof, and performing feats of magic, mind-reading, tightwire walking, bareback riding, juggling, being ventriloquists, or performing acrobatics. Vaudeville drew on all of the other performing arts and presented opera singers, ballet dancers, circus stars, sports champions, minstrels, serious musicians as well as some who stood on their heads as they played, Swiss bell-ringers, troupes of midgets from Germany, tumblers from Japan, Wild West shows, and the great stars of the legitimate theatre. It featured horses that could count, female impersonators, trained seals and skating bears, monologists, harmonica players, xylophonists, fire-eaters, unicyclists, and everything else that was new, startling, or sensational—and best of all, unbelievable.

For half a century vaudeville's children introduced and made popular most of the hit songs—some that are now perennial favourites. Vaudevillians also wrote their share of those hits, patriotic, topical, religious, comic. They were the first to sing the sentimental numbers about mothers, the girl left behind, and the charm of a humble childhood home being better than all of the world's gold. Later on they ushered in the age of syncopation, jazz, and the even wilder music of the twenties.

Although American vaudeville was presented to the public in a variety of locations, it was booked by only a few companies who owned or controlled a series of theatres, called a "circuit." These companies controlled the booking of vaudeville acts for their respective circuits and promoted tours of those acts across the continent. The Keith and Orpheum circuits dominated the eastern part of the United States, and presented "Big-Time" vaudeville, although the Keith Circuit also controlled a large number of "Small-Time" venues. Big-Time vaudeville meant that the performance would include several big-name acts on the same bill. There were typically two shows a day. The West Coast was dominated by the Pantages, Considine, and Loew's circuits, which offered Small-Time or "two-bit" vaudeville. This did not mean

A full-page personal invitation from Alexander Pantages to attend the opening of the Pantages appeared in the *Toronto Star Weekly*, August 28, 1920.

Pantages

AT last, a Pantages Theatre for Toronto. At last a mighty, colossal, magnificent structure surpassing in elegance, design and equipment all previous efforts in theatrical construction in all Canada.

At last, the introduction of the Pantages vaudeville, in Toronto, embracing the most carefully selected amusement that it is possible for experts to obtain.

At last the fulfillment of the dream I have cherished for a quarter of a century—that some day I might enter the eastern theatrical field, and there bring to a culmination the results of years of experience gained largely throughout the western portion of the continent.

The fond anticipation of this day has been mine since my first real effort on Canadian soil away back in the early days at Victoria, B.C. As the Pantages' organization expanded, as its influence became felt widely and yet more widely, as city after city came into that organization—yet it was not the climax I sought.

Today forty cities throughout Canada and the United States have a Pantages theatre. It remained for Toronto to have the greatest of these—the most expensive of these.

And over a million dollars have been spent in the erection of this palatial theatre.

A quarter of a century of conscientious effort has gone into the building of it. It has been built with a view to providing the maximum of comfort and convenience. It has been built to accommodate nearly 3,700 persons and a feature of its construction is this, that there is perfect vision from every chair. The advice of the best building experts money could employ was secured. The services of the most illustrious designers were brought into play. This theatre has been furnished by the most skilful master workmen; it has been equipped by those whose knowledge is the result of many years of scientific experience.

But best of all—it has been built for you. The Pantages theatre in Toronto has been made possible by the assistance and financial support of J. P. Bickell, N. L. Nathanson, and their associates, and this beautiful edifice is going to be a most wonderful incentive to me to present at all times the best entertainment that my thirty years of experience can provide. I want you to feel that it is yours, that all this effort and all this money has been expended for you, that you and yours may enjoy the entertainment offered to the very ultimate.

A close and lifelong study of human nature and the experience which I have gained because of catering to the amusement lovers of a continent, enables me to choose with accuracy the type of entertainment best suited to a general audience.

Many years ago, in the far west, I conceived the idea of giving people vaudeville shows at a small admission. This style of entertainment sprung into instant popularity. The masses and classes both flocked to the first Pantages theatre then, as they do in forty cities today.

As time progressed, I continued to improve my vaudeville until today I have come to the point where I firmly believe that no organization on the face of the earth is able to give as much real entertainment value for the money as are the Pantages theatres. Each act, number and feature is selected under my own personal direction and I take particular pains and care to see that each bill contains the ingredients that go to make a delightful entertainment embracing comedy, singing, dancing and novelty acts.

I-NOW-INVITE-YOU-TO-COME.

I know you will come. I know that you will come in thousands. I know that when the doors are opened wide on Monday that your response will be the greatest that has ever been witnessed at any previous time in the theatrical history of this, the Queen City of Canada.

This is my welcome to you.

It carries with it the sincere desires of one who earnestly requests that you participate in this unique success.

Nor does this welcome begin and end with the formal opening.

It extends to you and yours as long as my name is there. If circumstance prevents your attendance at the opening performance, it shall not deter you, I trust, from making this theatre your pleasure place as often as opportunity permits.

I assure you that each moment spent within the walls of the Pantages theatre will be moments to linger in memory—and I trust that they will endure when the dust of time will have silvered with the ages.

ALEXANDER PANTAGES

that the circuit itself was a two-bit operation, but that there was just one big-name act on the bill and that the price of admission was less than that for Big-Time vaudeville. To increase the revenue generated in these Small-Time houses, three or more shows were presented daily. Also, unlike Big-Time, Small-Time vaudeville sometimes showed movies along with the other acts. The vaudeville performed in Toronto closely resembled the two types of vaudeville enjoyed by its American neighbours to the south.

OPENING NIGHT

A gala opening was planned for the Toronto Pantages on Saturday, August 28, 1920. Because of the grandeur of the theatre itself, most show goers thought that the vaudeville acts would have to be exceptional in order to be selected to play there. This thinking was promoted by management in an advertisement in *The Evening Telegram* for the opening performance that announced: "A new page will be written in Toronto's theatrical history, and for a long time to come thousands and thousands will comment on the wondrous beauty of this exquisite palace of amusement."

The competition that weekend was significant. Just across town,

TO-NIGHT
at the
PANTAGES THEATRE

A new page will be written in Toronto's theatrical history, and for a long time to come, thousands and thousands will comment upon the wondrous beauty of this exquisite palace of amusement. To help in to-night's dedication exercises,

Montagu Love
and
Mildred Harris Chaplin

have journeyed to Toronto to lend their services on this occasion.

To-night, at 6.30, the management will expect to place on sale about 500 additional seats, but those who may be unable to gain admission will be able to witness the opening performance in its entirety all next week.

Starting Monday, performances will be continuous from 12 noon until 11 p.m. Matinee admissions—to 5 o'clock—will be 25c. After that hour tickets will be 45c.

A second newspaper ad promoted the opening night's guest stars.

the Royal Alexandra was presenting what proved to be one of the biggest hits of the 1920s, *Chu Chin Chow*. The famous Canadian comedy team, The Dumbells, was appearing at the Grand Opera House. Shea's Hippodrome, the Strand, and Loew's all had vaudeville programs that included films. As well, fourteen movie theatres were advertising programs of films only. Nevertheless, the Pantages' opening was apparently not overshadowed, for the reviews that followed were unrestrained in their accolades.

To begin the evening, Fred Radford conducted the large orchestra in a special overture, after which Mildred Harris Chaplin, film star and wife of Charlie Chaplin, was introduced and briefly expressed her pleasure at being in Canada, home of her mother's parents. The premier film performance that night featured Mrs. Chaplin and silent film star, Montagu Love. Six vaudeville acts completed the program. Maud Earl presented a novel act entitled "The Vocal Verdict." In it, she appeared in a court of justice, dressed as various characters. The audience acted as the jury and a judge passed sentence on her. Fred P. Allen, a clever young monologist, who originated all of his own material, appeared on stage for eighteen minutes before being replaced by the Marconi Brothers. Recognized in vaudeville circles as two of its cleverest entertainers, they were masters of the classical, standard, and jazz numbers they performed on the piano and the accordion. They closed, as always, to a house-rocking round of applause. McGrath and Deeds, two young men with better than ordinary voices, then sang several numbers. Marjorie Peterson headed the dance act, "Danse Divertissement," which consisted of six women, nearly all of whom had been on tour with the then famous Ted Shawn. Their series of dances ranged from the "Valse Ballet," a quaint little number danced in crinoline hoopskirts, to the "Danse Egyptiene," a more exotic entry. The last act, "On the High Seas," was a production that depicted life on the ocean during the war when submarines were a menace to shipping. One press account of "On the High Seas" advised the audience that there were eleven people in the acting company and a large corps of mechanicians behind the scenes. Another said that the act was hard to describe and that it was wonderful what could be done with stage effects and the proper use of lighting. It advised its readers to see "just what can be done by these ingenious people."

The Evening Telegram issue of Monday, August 30, 1920, described the success of that opening night: "Never before has a Toronto theatre had such a gala opening as the Pantages on Saturday night. The huge auditorium was packed. Hundreds of invited guests were in full dress. . . . Mayor Church delivered the dedicatory address and Sir Thomas Lipton [Lipton Tea empire] had a seat in one of the boxes."

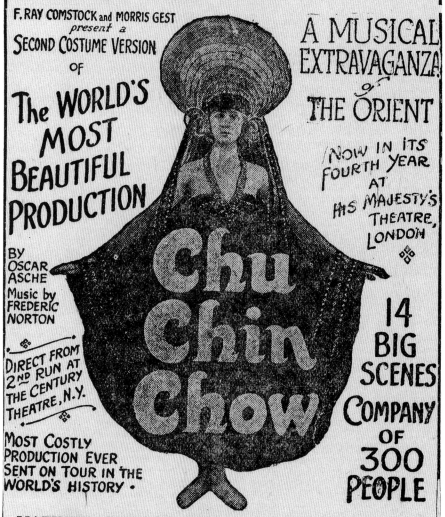

ALEXANDRA TWICE TO-DAY "HELLO ALEXANDER"

Commencing Next Monday Evening

AT 8 P.M. SHARP

Owing to enormous size of production, and length of performance, curtain rises promptly at 8 o'clock. Patrons are respectfully requested to be in their seats by that time, as POSITIVELY no one will be seated during the first scene.

F. RAY COMSTOCK and MORRIS GEST present a SECOND COSTUME VERSION OF

The WORLD'S MOST BEAUTIFUL PRODUCTION

BY OSCAR ASCHE Music by FREDERIC NORTON

DIRECT FROM 2ND RUN AT THE CENTURY THEATRE, N.Y.

MOST COSTLY PRODUCTION EVER SENT ON TOUR IN THE WORLD'S HISTORY

A MUSICAL EXTRAVAGANZA of THE ORIENT

NOW IN ITS FOURTH YEAR AT HIS MAJESTY'S THEATRE, LONDON

Chu Chin Chow

14 BIG SCENES COMPANY OF 300 PEOPLE

MATINEES WEDNESDAY AND SATURDAY AT 2 P.M.
Nights—$1.00, $1.50, $2.00, $2.50 and $3.00
Wed. Mat.—$1.00, $1.50 and $2.00
Sat. Mat.—$1.00, $1.50, $2.00 and $2.50
FAREWELL PRESENTATION IN THIS CITY

When the Pantages opened its doors on August 28, 1920, one of its competitors, the Royal Alexandra, was showing one of the most successful musicals of the decade, *Chu Chin Chow*.

AN EVENING AT THE PANTAGES

After the gala opening of the Pantages, shows were changed biweekly. When the opening show moved on, it was replaced with a program that included, as its premier attraction, *Past, Present, and Future*, a comedy based on the high cost of living. Then followed The Great Leon & Company, exponents of Hindu magic, and Charles Olcott, who offered "a pianologue guaranteed to please everyone." Ed Blondell & Co. presented a funny sketch entitled "The Boy from Home," and Mary Ann sang a number of character songs. The Three Sons of Jazz with their novelty singing, dancing, and instrumental number preceded the feature picture — Dorothy Dalton in *Guilty of Love*. A Hank Mann comedy entitled *Who's Your Grocer?* and the Pantages' *Pictorial Review* completed the bill.

It must be remembered that the Pantages' programming was Small-Time vaudeville and thus did not include the big stars of Broadway or New York's Big-Time vaudeville. The Small-Time performers travelled the Pantages Circuit throughout the western United States, then western Canada and Toronto. A New York performer would occasionally headline at the Pantages, as happened in November of 1920. Al Shayne, known as "The Singing Beauty," played the Pantages direct from successful appearances in New York, which included *Cinderella on Broadway* and *Shubert's Gaieties of 1919*.

By the early 1920s, the format for vaudeville and movie presentations had become well entrenched. The show would begin with an acrobatic, pantomime, or animal act, often called a "flash act." This act was at a disadvantage because the audience often was still being seated during its presentation. The headliner was positioned immediately before intermission because this was considered to be the most desirable spot on the bill. Intermission was followed by several lesser acts. The last position on the bill, like the first, was not very desirable from the performers' point of view because people sometimes left the theatre before the last act was finished.

The first part of an evening at the Pantages would have been something like this one described by theatre-organ enthusiast Izz Gang: "The evening would begin with the overture played by a 24-piece theatre orchestra, followed by orchestral selections from Faust, *News of the Week* on film, and a movie comedy, perhaps Charlie Chaplin in *The Cure*. Next in line would be a singsong with the Mighty Wurlitzer." Words to each song would be projected on the screen (a picture sheet, as it was called) and the audience would be directed as to how to sing the words by a bouncing ball. If a note was to be sung high, then the ball would bounce high; if it was to be sung low, the ball would fall.

One presentation was very significant to me. It was the time when our beloved Mary Pickford appeared in a play called The Little Churchmouse. *My chum and I each purchased an autograph book at Woolworth's, and when the play was over we dashed around to the Victoria Street stage door where a small crowd had gathered. When Mary emerged she smiled and spoke to us, then entered her limo where she sat for a while and graciously signed autographs. I've kept this autograph ever since among my souvenirs.*

Anna Bailey, Pantages' patron

It was not unusual for a number of the acts, the theatre organist, the master of ceremonies, or the orchestra leader to involve the audience in direct participation. A devoted patron of the Pantages, Syd Moyle of Rexdale, recounts a poignant scene involving a member of the audience:

After the conclusion of World War I, the Pantages was the place to go in Toronto, which was then a very pro-British and patriotic town. Frank Richardson, a friend of my parents, had just returned home from hospital, having been wounded in the battle of Ypres in France. He had sustained a direct hit that took his leg off just above the knee. He and his mates, still in uniform, went to see the show at the Pantages. Frank was gifted with a beautiful voice and, unknown to him, one of his pals had approached the show's master of ceremonies in the men's room and told him of Frank's talents and of his recent return from the hospital. Richardson was of course unaware of the plot until he was summoned backstage by the master of ceremonies. After he got over the initial shock, he agreed to sing a very popular hit of that era, "I'm Always Chasing Rainbows."

His friends in attendance described the scenario to my parents: "There he stood on one leg supported by a single crutch, in full uniform, a nervous smile on his face. A rather forlorn and pathetic picture, reduced to a tiny figure by that mammoth stage and the glare of a single spotlight, on stage 'front and centre' at the famous Pantages, Canada's most prestigious theatre. He soon won the sympathy of the audience. He sang like a soul possessed. The ladies in the crowd were openly sobbing and even hardened veterans were fighting back tears. The old troopers who 'walked the boards' on the Buffalo-Toronto circuit said they had never heard a spontaneous ovation like it."

Motion pictures, though not necessarily the best ones, were another important part of the show at the Pantages. Many of the famous people the audiences saw there in the flesh had performed in

Some of the many talented men and women who performed at the Pantages between 1920 and 1929. The Pantages could attract the best performers and, as a result, the quality of the stage performances was very high.

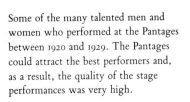

movies. In the beginning, it was not at all unusual for the show on the stage to be far better than the one on the silent screen. But by 1923, motion picture feature presentations had become the headliners, and the vaudeville acts followed them on the playbill.

In 1925, the music of the Wurlitzer, with or without any audience participation, would be followed by the Prologue, an extended series of short films, and a feature presentation, such as Lon Chaney in *The Phantom of the Opera*. This might be followed by a cartoon or a novelty, a short film based on a popular novel of the day. And finally the vaudeville show began, with six acts, one after another. The entire show would then repeat itself. Sometimes the show on the stage would be integrated to some extent with the one on the screen. These "unit" shows travelled around a theatre circuit in conjunction with the movie presentation.

Unlike today, the audience was not expected to leave when the show ended. If they thought part of the show was worth seeing again, they could stay, and many did. Nor did the vaudeville theatres have a policy of asking everyone to be in their seats before the show started. People came in or left at any time during the stage show or the movie. Usually, however, they had the courtesy to stay in their seats until the applause was over, or at least until a vaudeville act ended. To encourage people to leave, the show would usually end with a short film that was so bad that it would clear the audience. These short films, because of their effectiveness, were affectionately referred to as chasers.

The quality of the stage performances at the Pantages was very high because the theatre could attract the best performers. Archie Leach, who later called himself Cary Grant, was one of the early ones. Leach, through his father's initiative, was adopted by Robert and Margaret Lomas, who headed up The Flying Penders. This famous British troupe of stilt-walkers and acrobatic dancers specialized in pantomime productions. By the time he was seven, Archie was being tossed around the stage of the Paris Olympia Theatre and the Berlin Winter Garden. It was this early beginning that led him to become a professional stilt-walker. After a stint with the Ringling Bros Circus in the United States, he joined the Lomas Troupe and played the Pantages Circuit several times between 1920 and 1925.

Much of the mystique and charm of vaudeville, and certainly an important part of the Pantages' experience, was provided by the theatre orchestra. The orchestra at the Pantages was under the skilled and very talented direction of Fred Radford for the years from 1920 to 1929. A quiet and reserved man, Radford was an excellent conductor who quickly established a standard of musical excellence. In addition

Dad never forgot Archie Leach. He was a very gregarious sort of person who liked people; apparently he was very nice to work with. He was a stiltwalker with the Lomas Vaudeville Troop. They had a great balancing and juggling act. In one comedy bit at the Pantages, Cary Grant played the rear end of a horse! After midnight one night after the show, the cast went to Child's Restaurant (as they often did) which was just a little further down Yonge Street, and Archie Leach entertained everybody by doing handstands on the table after he had finished his coffee and dessert. Dad thought he was a very friendly and easygoing person.

Joe Radford, son of Pantages' orchestra leader Fred Radford

to being a talented violinist, he was also a skilled sight-reader. This was particularly useful in vaudeville because many of the acts would present the orchestra leader with their own handwritten sheet music and expect a professional performance with very little rehearsal. Then, too, some of the silent movies would have a prepared score, which only added to the copious amounts of new music that were constantly being placed in front of the theatre's orchestra. Because of the tremendous public demand, the orchestra was expected to play three, sometimes four, or even five shows a day. The amount of rehearsal time was even more severely restricted when, as was often the case, the show opened with a movie before noon and closed after the last show at 11:00 p.m. There was no show on Sunday, but the orchestra seldom practised then anyway—not in "Toronto the Good."

Fred Radford was the leader of the Pantages' orchestra throughout its vaudeville years. He was a gifted conductor who, having read a score once, could conduct the orchestra with little or no hesitation. The high standard of musical excellence achieved at the Pantages was largely the result of his talent and dedication.

Colleen Moore [one of the great silent film stars] was a very big hit at the theatre. I guess she came through to plug her movie, but she sure impressed me. I know now that she later became a great friend of Lillian Gish, but at the time, I was so in love with her that I wrote her a letter. Right after I met her, I wrote this letter backstage at the theatre — I was only a kid — to tell her how great she was. I am sad to say, she never answered. That was the only time either of us [he and his brother] tried to keep in contact with the stars who came to the Pantages.

•

We all heard about the electrician who had the misfortune to kill the spotlight too quickly on Lupe Valez [a temperamental Hollywood film star]. On her way off the stage in the semi-darkness, the "Mexican Spitfire" ripped out a huge hatpin which held some of the huge feathers to her headdress, and jabbed him square in the behind saying . . . 'that's the last time you'll ever do that to me young man!' Unfortunately, the rest of the stage lights were not all turned off, nor was the microphone, so the audience saw and heard the whole thing. They loved it!

•

We made great friends with "Scooter" Lowery, one of the original Our Gang Comedy *boys. He was a drummer in vaudeville and had his own solo act when he was maybe ten or eleven. He was just an ordinary, unaffected kid, who was lonely being on the road all the time. We played tag with him backstage. We used to run along the great airhoses that were connected up to the vacuum system. The stagehands used to clean and vacuum the stage while the movie was on. The three of us drove the stagehands nuts by running back and forth from one side of the stage to the other along these hoses. We had a lot of fun with him while he was in Toronto, and he told us that it meant a lot to him to hang around with us.*

Joe Radford, son of Pantages' orchestra leader Fred Radford

When it opened, the Pantages Theatre stated its programming policy as follows: "The bills will include six unequalled vaudeville acts, features, photoplays, and an admirable selection of film comedies, news reels, and scenics." In 1929, the Pantages was still presenting "five great acts of vaudeville and *Black Waters*, the sensational 100% all-talking melodrama." However, most American theatres had given up live shows by the end of the twenties. The big Deluxe Publix unit shows were disbanded on October 29, 1929. Only the great flagship houses in large metropolitan areas, such as the Chicago Theatre, the New York Paramount, and a sprinkling of others continued.

Unfortunately for Alexander Pantages, he realized too late the importance of movies as part of his programming, and failed to buy or align himself with a movie production company. His more astute competitors, on the other hand, made exclusive arrangements with all of the important motion picture distributors. The Loew's Circuit, for example, which had also presented Small-Time vaudeville,

Advertisement in the *Toronto Star Weekly* on July 6, 1929 announcing the 100% "All Talking" moving picture.

pioneered in the presentation of motion pictures in its theatres. It ended up in common ownership with Metro Goldwyn Mayer, which produced the most prestigious films of the 1930s. By the time sound came to the movies and finished off vaudeville in the process, the Pantages Circuit was unable to book "blockbuster" movies. These went to other circuits. Consequently, the Pantages Theatre had far too many empty seats as the 1920s came to a close. In late 1927, Eastern Theatres Limited, which had managed the theatre up to that time, amalgamated its operations with the Famous Players Canadian Corporation. Almost concurrently, Pantages sold his six largest theatres on the West Coast to RKO (Radio-Keith-Orpheum) and Warner Brothers, and the circuit quickly disintegrated. The next year, shortly after highly publicized, although subsequently unproven, charges were laid against Alexander Pantages for child molestation and rape, his name was taken down from every marquee in Canada.

On March 15, 1930, the Pantages officially became the Imperial Theatre. It continued to offer first-class live shows for a while. Its vaudeville acts came from the Orpheum Circuit, owned by RKO, which also owned a large motion picture production company in Hollywood. The Imperial became the flagship of Famous Players and staged more elaborate and expensive shows than almost any other vaudeville theatre on the continent.

The nearby Loew's was the first of Toronto's vaudeville theatres to drop live performances. It had offered vaudeville upstairs in the Winter Garden sporadically until 1928 when the decision was made to close the upstairs theatre completely rather than equip it for sound. Shea's Hippodrome, which by 1931 was advertising itself as "Shea's — Canada's Foremost Vaudeville Theatre," was still offering "first-class vaudeville and a movie." The Imperial converted to an all-movie policy in 1935 after all of the other Toronto vaudeville houses but Shea's had already done so. Shea's offered special live shows off and on as late as the 1940s and was the last of the vaudeville/movie theatres to give up live entertainment entirely.

All through the '30s, the '40s, and even the '50s, MGM was Hollywood's greatest studio. The Shea's and Famous Players' houses could not get these pictures until Loew's was finished showing them, which could be many months or even years. Obviously there was not the same need for Loew's to offer live entertainment, as the drawing power of its films was enough.

At the Imperial, however, RKO's films, such as *Doctors' Wives*, with Warner Baxter and Joan Bennett, were accompanied by an edition of the Publix Unit Revue, a musical performance that was specially written and directed to complement the film. This elaborate stage

In the beginning years of the Pantages, the organ and the orchestra played together, but later the organ, which could provide all the sounds of the orchestra and more, replaced it. Kathleen Stokes was one of the organists at the newly renamed Imperial Theatre. She later became well known as a member of the famous "Happy Gang" radio show.

The Shea's Hippodrome, built on the west side of Bay Street where the new Toronto City Hall now stands, accommodated 3,000 customers.

Advertisement in the *Toronto Star Weekly* on February 7, 1931 announcing the return of famous musical director and producer Jack Arthur's Imperialettes.

production provided by RKO was sent around its entire North American circuit. The Imperial would, therefore, present the same show that would have appeared at the world's largest theatre, now the RKO Roxy. A Publix Revue Unit program looked something like this:

"Westward Ho"
with
JACK PEPPER
"Making Whoppee"
QUEEN, QUEEN AND QUEEN
"Three of a kind doing something different"
CALIFORNIA CROONERS
"Western Melodies"
CARLTON EMMY AND HIS WAGS
"Applause Going to the Dogs"
LUCILLE PETERSEN
"Voice of the Golden West"
RUSSELL MARKERT GIRLS

The glorious days of vaudeville came to an end partly because of the shortage of good acts to fill the thousands of theatres all over North America. Audiences quickly spotted second-rate performances, especially when they could compare them to great performances they might have seen the week before in the same theatre. Not only that, the onset of new technology was bringing the vaudeville stars and memorable songs directly into the home. Both local radio and network broadcasting made it possible to stay at home and hear vaudeville greats, many of whom were now performing "on the air."

The freshness of vaudeville became a thing of the past. If an act had been featured on radio, its appeal was greatly diluted. Indeed, radio consumed and aged material faster than the writers and performers could produce it. Most of the great music and comedy routines were adapted for radio or the movies with lightning speed. And as radio developed, theatre audiences matured and became more discriminating. In the end, if they hadn't heard of an act, then perhaps it wasn't worth the price of admission at a theatre. However, the coup de grâce was dealt by the movies. The introduction of sound and the technical improvements that were constantly being made to the medium proved to be an unbeatable combination.

The decline of vaudeville was swift indeed. Big-Time vaudeville was the first to die, and between the years of 1928 to 1930, it had all but disappeared. Small-Time vaudeville, which had always included film, survived somewhat longer.

It is hard to believe that it was back in the thirties when all of that extravagant and unique splendour came to an end with the demise of vaudeville. Even though moving pictures continued to be presented in the same environment for a good number of years, it was a totally different ambience to the vitality and the sense of dramatic expectancy which the vaudeville performers and the live orchestra brought to each and every performance, week in and week out, every time the curtain went up.

Joe Radford, son of Pantages' orchestra leader Fred Radford

The advertisement for the Jack Arthur Christmas show announces the elaborate presentation that would precede the feature film. The choral ensemble for "Mothers of the World" included 25 performers who sang and danced to the accompaniment of the orchestra. The audience then enjoyed the weekly newsreel, a cartoon and the feature starring Bing Crosby in a comedy.

Joe Radford, son of the Pantages orchestra leader Fred Radford, recounts how sudden and difficult the demise of vaudeville was for performers. His aunt, Viola Ellis, of the team Ellis and West, a popular dance team, told him what it meant to her and her friends: "The advent of the 'talkies,' followed by the Depression, was devastating to the many entertainers who had no training or skills of a more practical nature on which to rely. Tommy Ellis, once a vaudeville star for many years, became a clown at Christmastime in the toyland of the old Queen Street Eaton's store. He also took part in the Santa Claus parade, and to my knowledge was responsible for appearing to walk the whole route on his hands! The upward-reaching legs harnessed to his shoulders apparently were his invention." But these jobs were slim pickings. Canada's famous O'Connor Sisters, Big-Time vaudeville's only "6-count-'em-6" singing sisters, went from filling the 5,000-seat Fox Theatre in Detroit for seventeen full weeks, to running a coffee shop at Toronto's Woodbine Race Track.

In 1932, although the regular vaudeville show had ceased at the Imperial, and the feature film presentation was now the headliner, the theatre still combined stage shows with its movies. Margaret Morrison, a talented singer, spent many happy hours at the Imperial in 1932 singing in orchestra leader Jack Arthur's chorus. She had trained at the Royal Conservatory of Music and, after auditions, landed a job at the Imperial. She remembers how thrilled she was with her first paycheque, $25 per week for singing in three shows a day.

The years that followed saw personal appearances by stars promoting their movies or selling war bonds, but the great Pantages' stage was used less and less. This is not to say that the life of the Imperial Theatre was uneventful. As the flagship of Famous Players Theatres, it witnessed many a premiere. Cinemascope, Stereosound, and many other motion picture developments were featured first in

Torontonian Margaret Morrison was one of the chorus girls who performed during the Imperial's Christmas show in 1933, in a Prelude called "Mothers of the World."

I loved the story Jack Arthur [the Imperial's orchestra leader] told me about the time he was rehearsing at the Imperial when things were not going at all well. He flew into a rage and yelled at the entire cast, throwing his watch onto the floor of the stage for emphasis. It smashed to bits and the cast, of course, was horrified. "There, see what you made me do!" he shouted. They were all terribly apologetic and quickly got their act together. But what they didn't know was that the watch was some cheap thing that he was about to throw out anyway.

He was a great musician and often conducted with his violin under his arm. I became great friends with his wife Midge as well. She was an excellent choreographer and was responsible for the Imperialettes, the theatre's famous kick-line.

Dorothy Bromby, Toronto theatre organist and conductor

I loved to sit high up in the balcony [of the Imperial] — even in the last few rows. With that great screen, the scope of the movie was not lost, and I loved the quiet and the lack of distraction that the back of the balcony offered. I always tried to sit alone so that I would not be disturbed. One afternoon a couple of elegantly dressed women in expensive-looking fur coats decided to sit near me and talk loudly all the way through the picture. I tapped one nervously on the shoulder and politely asked if she would mind not speaking so loudly. They both were so incensed by this that they called an usher and tried to have the manager "throw this crackpot out" for ruining their appreciation of the movie!

The Imperial was a great place to see a movie and was one of my favourites. As a critic, I saw so many movies that I never was able to remember where I saw a particular film, but I do recall the splendour of that vast auditorium.

Clyde Gilmour, movie critic and radio personality

In 1970, Buddy Rogers, husband of renowned Hollywood actress Mary Pickford, came to Toronto to present a revival of Miss Pickford's *Pollyanna* at the Imperial Theatre.

Canada's largest movie theatre. And for years the Imperial was the country's top-grosser. The orchestra pit was cemented over so that a few more rows of seats could be added, and the theatre organ was sealed forever. Even with the box seats unused, the seating capacity was a Toronto record of 3,626.

The theatre's stage was used for the last time in 1969, when Buddy Rogers, who was then married to Mary Pickford, came to town to present a revival of *Pollyanna*. The red carpet was rolled out and the kleig lights shone once again to welcome the capacity crowd to see the movie. Rogers walked onto the stage to give an emotional introduction to the old hit by Toronto's own Mary Pickford, "America's Sweetheart." Horace Lapp accompanied the movie on a specially installed electric theatre organ. The pristine print was shown on the gigantic original vertical format screen, the top portion of which had been covered for years with black cloth to give it the length and width necessary for today's movies. It was a memorable evening, entirely suitable for the theatre's final stage appearance by a star. The theatre saw two more renovations and two more marquees before it was split into smaller auditoriums. Unfortunately, each renovation was less attractive than the one before it.

Although it may not have been so aesthetically pleasing to look at as it once was, the fact is that the Imperial was more successful than ever. In June of 1972, it set its own new record with the playing of *The Godfather*, which had a run of over sixteen weeks and grossed over $800,000. It was the last regular commercial motion picture to be shown in the single-screen Imperial.

On September 4, 1972, at the age of fifty-two years, the doors to the Imperial Theatre closed, and its existence as a single-auditorium movie palace ended. The same forces that were at work to usher out vaudeville, also ushered out the movie palace. Just as the presentation of movies in the late 1920s reduced the costs of a theatre that had previously shown only vaudeville acts, so, too, presenting four or more films under one roof would prove to be more economical than showing just one. In the early 1970s, the single-auditorium theatre was becoming an anachronism, as the number of available movies and venues diluted the audience for these grand showcases. The multiplex cinema allowed an owner to spread his financial risk over a number of films. If one proved unsuccessful, there was always the possibility that another would be a hit.

And so Canada's largest movie house, the Imperial Theatre, underwent its next metamorphosis by changing from a single auditorium to a sixplex. The $2-million reconstruction took approximately eleven months to complete, and the Imperial Six reopened on June 21, 1973.

Toronto born actress, Mary Pickford, whose illustrious career spanned four decades, often delighted the Pantages' audience.

I was the baby in a family of five, but when I was about ten years old, I was allowed to go to the Pickford Theatre at the corner of Queen and Spadina. I loved to watch The Perils of Pauline *and other serials for the bargain price of five cents. I often stayed until a slide was projected on the screen which told the audience that if they left immediately they would receive a grab bag as a gift — otherwise, half the crowd would have stayed all day and the management would not have been able to sell more tickets. The handsome older gentleman who was the manager was always there, as was the no-nonsense matron who kept us all quiet in our seats. Mom and Dad always felt we were safe at the Pickford and encouraged us to go to "our" theatre. For this reason, I really was not very aware of what the big downtown theatres were like.*

One day when I was eleven years old, my sister-in-law took me on the streetcar across town to the Pantages Theatre. Walking up the beautiful long entrance to the grand lobby filled me with awe, but when I descended that grand staircase, a wonderful feeling came over me. I felt that when I was on the streetcar, I was a child, but as I began to descend that grand staircase, I somehow had suddenly grown into a young lady. It was an amazing feeling that I shall not forget.

Recently, when I was lucky enough to be taken on a private tour of the darkened theatre and I walked down that same luxurious staircase in the half-light, that wonderful feeling came rushing back to me. It was as if a lifetime had flashed by in a single magical moment.

Ida Clarfield, Pantages' patron

A THEATRE RESTORED

The reconstruction of the Imperial Theatre into six smaller auditoriums within the same space reflected the trend that was sweeping through North America's entertainment industry in the 1960s and 1970s. These beautiful old monuments were undergoing conversions from large single houses into smaller multiple cinemas, and the architectural integrity of their original structure and design was being destroyed.

When Cineplex Odeon Corporation, a Canadian company, acquired its first American circuit in 1985, its chief executive officer, Garth H. Drabinsky, bore witness to these desecrations as he toured the company's new theatre chain. It disturbed him to see formerly magnificent picture palaces now converted into poorly split multiple auditoriums, bingo halls, parking garages and sometimes "houses of ill repute." Even more of them had been boarded up waiting for their final demolition to make way for new developments. Mr. Drabinsky was concerned that far too little was being done to preserve those that remained, and he committed himself and his company to the restoration wherever feasible of any of the company's newly acquired theatres that possessed architectural or cultural merit.

So when the opportunity arose to purchase the Imperial Six in May, 1986, Mr. Drabinsky decided not only to proceed with the purchase, but to determine whether or not it would be possible to recapture the theatre's original splendour. Initially, Cineplex Odeon was only able to purchase one half of the complex and construction began on the renovation of the single-screened cinema on October 2, 1987. It ended on December 11, 1987, when the theatre reopened under its original name, the Pantages.

While he was carefully following the progress of this first reconstruction, however, Mr. Drabinsky began to regret more and more that the theatre's true potential would be only partly realized by the conversion of half of it into a single-auditorium motion picture theatre. He became convinced that the whole building could be made into a

The completely restored upper lobby of the Pantages theatre.

A new concession counter was installed in the upper lobby during the 1987 renovation and was flanked by some of the original columns from 1920.

stunning success, both aesthetically and commercially, if it could be returned to one ownership and then carefully restored as a venue for live theatre. He was, of course, mindful of how few such venues there were in Toronto and of how receptive Toronto audiences were to live theatre. He was also aware of the critical and public acclaim he and his company had already achieved in restoring theatres in Los Angeles and Manhattan.

He therefore arranged a meeting with David Mesbur and Peter Kofman, the architect and the engineer who were overseeing the conversion. After telling them the direction his thoughts were taking, he asked them to obtain the original plans of the building and then to carry out a thorough analysis of what would be necessary not only to restore but, to convert the Pantages to a theatre capable of staging elaborate productions for an audience large enough to make the restoration economically feasible. Messrs. Mesbur and Kofman reported back in due course, having studied all of the existing data and consulted with experts in live-theatre design in New York and elsewhere. With extensive structural modifications the former vaudeville house could be converted to a theatre capable of accommodating drama, opera, and ballet. The estimated $18-million renovation would mean that the new structure would then have the ability to attract world-class productions, and could thus be economically viable.

Just one month after the reopening of the Pantages Theatre as a single screen cinema, Cineplex Odeon established a live entertainment division to produce and present stage productions in Toronto. Its presentations of *Macbeth*, with Glenda Jackson and Christopher Plummer, *Me and My Girl*, with Tim Curry, and *Cabaret*, with Joel Grey, had been met with critical acclaim and sold-out houses at the O'Keefe Centre. It also confirmed that the demand for top-quality live entertainment obviously still existed in the city.

The potential of the live entertainment division and the ability to

A view of the lobby after it was renovated in 1987, with its grand staircase and Joyce Wieland's massive painting entitled "Celebration."

create a world-class theatre from the Pantages prompted Mr. Drabinsky to start negotiations for the other half of the theatre. He was not surprised to find that the owner, Famous Players, would be reluctant to sell if the premises were to be used to present motion pictures in competition with its own outlets, but that any other use would be permitted. In April, 1988 the purchase was completed and plans were started for the reconstruction and restoration of the whole building. Live entertainment would once again appear on the Pantages' stage.

Although it was now possible to begin the restoration, there was still much concern about the financial risk inherent in a project of this magnitude. All other restorations of the grand movie palaces of the past were either spearheaded or financially subsidized by governmental authorities because in very few instances had a restoration and operation of a theatre this size proven to be economically feasible. The Pantages would represent the largest private restoration of its kind.

The initial challenge, and one that would determine whether or not the Pantages would see and sustain live entertainment on its stage, was then to ensure the economic viability of the theatre. Mr. Drabinsky was convinced that a blockbuster production, if acquired within the first years of operation of the theatre, would cover both its own

Interior of the renovated 900-seat cinema with the partially exposed dome as it appeared in 1987. This space was once a portion of the original theatre's balcony. The restored wall murals on each side of the auditorium are two parts of the original three-part wall mural which hung on the curved soundboard above the stage. Unfortunately, the central portion of the mural no longer exists.

running costs and the amortization of the restoration costs throughout its extended production run. The timing proved to be in favour of the project, as the phenomenally successful London and Broadway musical *The Phantom of the Opera* had not yet been licensed for presentation in Canada. Mr. Drabinsky contacted The Really Useful Group in London, England, and in June, 1988, after much negotiation, Cineplex Odeon secured the rights to *The Phantom of the Opera*.

Reconstruction and restoration of the Pantages began in the fall of 1988. Thus came about the costliest and most extensive non-government-funded theatre restoration ever attempted in recent history. And thus was the newly renovated Pantages Cinema doomed to a lifetime of only nine months, from December, 1987 to August, 1988.

To reintroduce the Pantages name to the public in 1987, a new neon and backlit marquee and new art deco stained-glass windows were designed for the Victoria Street facade. The signage and marquee were removed during the 1989 restoration.

THE RESTORATION BEGINS

Mr. Drabinsky had two objectives for the construction of the Pantages that would result in its establishment as a world-class contemporary live theatre. The first was to reconstruct the Pantages so that it would be capable of accommodating the most extravagant productions from Broadway and/or London's West End. The second was to return the Pantages to its original 1920s splendour by restoring those few original elements that had somehow escaped destruction over the years. In areas where this was not possible, the original components would be recreated with the approval of the Toronto Historical Board and within the acceptable limits of today's building codes.

To ensure that the restoration and any necessary re-creation were completely accurate, the original drawings of Thomas Lamb, the architect who designed the theatre in 1919, were obtained from Columbia University in New York City. These were vital to the understanding of the building's layout and its detailing, and to the correct interpretation of much of the information gathered from the research undertaken for the theatre's 1987 refurbishment. A significant number of details and construction elements had been restored as part of the earlier renovation.

The same companies that had worked on the reconstruction of the single auditorium a year earlier — the Mesbur and Kofman organizations and the contractor Execway Construction Ltd. — now took on the much more formidable complete restoration. They put together a team of professionals, all specializing in their respective disciplines, and immediately began the task of identifying the functional, electrical, mechanical, structural, acoustical, and life safety requirements.

The team faced numerous problems, including an acute shortage of manpower resulting from the heavy demand for labourers and skilled craftspeople in the Toronto construction industry's boom years of 1988 and 1989. The time frame for a restoration of this size and complexity was painfully short, but had been dictated by two events. The first was the acquisition of the remainder of the property in April, 1988, and the second was the scheduled opening of the Toronto production of *The Phantom of the Opera* in September, 1989. This meant a mere fifteen months for the completion of the project, because two months were needed for the installation of the elaborate production set for the musical and for the rehearsal of the cast.

To overcome these serious time constraints, a construction crew of 150 was hired, and the project schedule was condensed by using what in the construction trade is known as "fast tracking." This meant that the demolition of much of the interior was started prior to the completion of the reconstruction drawings and that construction

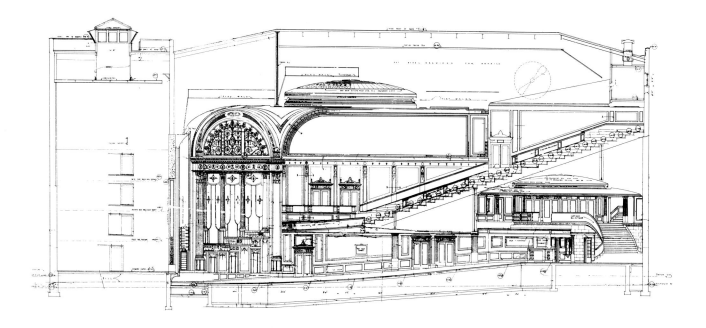

was begun while the building shell was still being measured. Every
component of the work proceeded concurrently. The normal construction sequence was constantly altered and modified to accommodate
the specialized needs of various project components. For example, the
finishing trades involved in painting, restoration, and marbleizing
were on site at the same time as the heavy construction trades, who
were working on the excavation, underpinning, and concrete work.
While heavy machinery was excavating and resupporting existing
foundations, craftspeople working on a temporary platform forty feet
in the air were applying gold leaf to the restored theatre dome above
the main auditorium. Against formidable odds and seemingly insur-
mountable difficulties, the work was completed on schedule.

To redesign and rebuild the theatre to meet the requirements of
today's more elaborate stage productions, and to incorporate the new
technology available to a first-class theatre, were both considerable
challenges. The task was complicated by the 1972 renovation, which
had significantly altered the structure of the building. Large portions
of the balcony had been removed to make way for exit passageways,
and all of the supporting steel for the box seats and much of the
structural framing around the proscenium had been cut out to improve
the screen sizes and seating capacity of the six auditoriums.

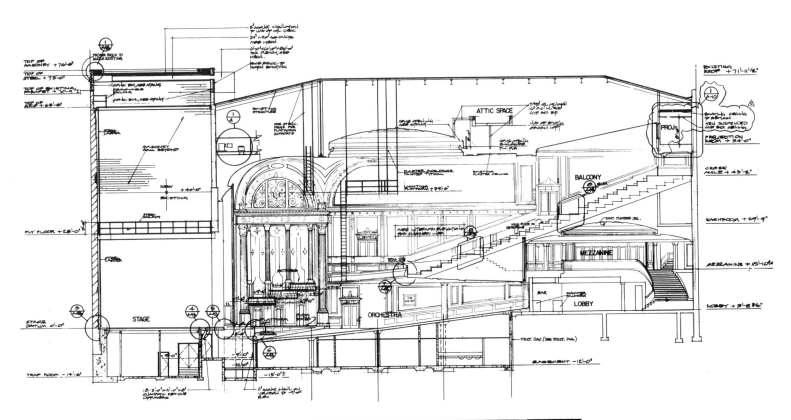

Using Thomas Lamb's cross-section as a guide, David Mesbur, the architect for the restoration, incorporated extensive modifications to the stage, auditorium and dressing rooms.

Massive excavation and underpinning of existing footings below the auditorium floor were required for the construction of dressing rooms and the installation of other backstage facilities.

A wide-angle view of the theatre as
seen from the stage during its
reconstruction. In 1972, this area was
subdivided into six separate cinemas.

But, in fact, the limitations of the Pantages as a live theatre venue went back to its very beginnings. The Pantages was initially constructed as a vaudeville theatre whose structure could not accommodate the more demanding needs of contemporary, live theatrical productions. The original vaudeville stage, although having an adequate depth of over thirty-four feet (as compared, for example, the Elgin Theatre's twenty-nine feet and the Royal Alexandra's thirty-five feet), had limited wing space which had been used for both the storage of props and for dressing rooms. There was little reason for a larger storage area for a vaudeville stage, as few props were then needed. The stage wings were extended to the limits of the property on the east and west and would be used exclusively for the additional storage of props. The height of the original stage, of approximately fifty-six feet, was adequate for 1920, since the backdrops were often simply painted curtains. However, to accommodate the size, complexity and sophistication of contemporary sets and props, the stage tower and grid were raised by approximately ten feet. To avoid destabilizing the structural walls of the stage tower, the original roof beams were left in place for lateral bracing and used to support the new grid floor.

By excavating sixteen feet below the auditorium floor, an entire underground level was constructed, which now contains dressing rooms for a cast of seventy, maintenance areas, sound equipment, electrical rooms, and other service areas. A fourteen-foot-deep trap

Today's advanced stage technology required the raising of the stage tower roof by approximately ten feet. On the left of the photograph, the extent of the new construction can be seen above the somewhat lower roof of the original dressing rooms. All of this space has been incorporated into the new stage tower. The additional height was needed to increase the fly space for the many elaborate sets that must be stored above the stage and "flown" in when needed.

room was built under the stage floor, incorporating an additional two-and-a-half-foot deep trench to hold a particular set piece for *The Phantom of the Opera*. An orchestra pit was built for forty musicians, with a pit lift that would automatically raise the orchestra floor to either auditorium floor level, stage level, or any other level that might be required by a specific production. As the original theatre footings were too shallow to accommodate the new basement area, extensive underpinning was required, and this had to be done with great care so as not to damage the fine plasterwork in the auditorium.

Working with theatre consultant Roger Morgan of New York City, new theatrical systems for riggings, traps, rakes, and stage areas were designed. The old hemp-rope and sand-bag rigging for stage backdrops was replaced by a modern counterweight system. Fly floor platforms were constructed on each side of the stage, and a new fire curtain and main draw were installed. The new fully trapped stage floor now accommodates the 190 trap doors necessary for the spectacular scenic effects of *The Phantom of the Opera*. Because the theatre was designed as a commercial facility, other elements were added such as a set of traps, light bridges, and other theatrical systems that will support future commercial productions. The result of these structural modifications is that the backstage is now superior to any theatre on Broadway.

The increased width of the stage meant that the rake of the balcony and the sight lines for the whole auditorium had to be modified. Both the auditorium's orchestra and balcony floor were resloped to improve

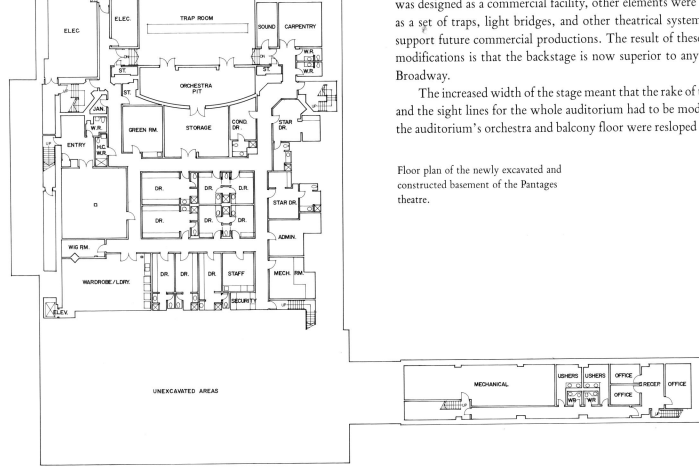

Floor plan of the newly excavated and constructed basement of the Pantages theatre.

sight lines dramatically and to allow for more generous seating space.

Unlike the original theatre, the new Pantages required a lobby, which had to be constructed within the existing framework. A lobby was designed at the bottom of the grand staircase, in the space that was formerly occupied by the back rows of the original auditorium. The distance from the stage to the last row of the orchestra was thereby reduced to only eighty-six feet, and the distance to the back row of the balcony was reduced by approximately ten feet, thus creating a more intimate relationship between the audience and the performers.

Modernization of the theatre also included the addition of coat-check rooms, an extra box office, and expanded and updated washroom facilities. Wider exitways were built to reflect current building-code

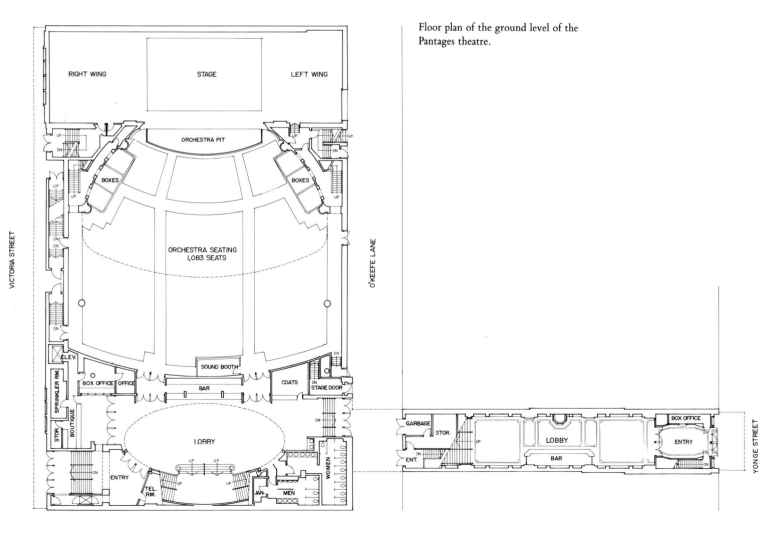

Floor plan of the ground level of the Pantages theatre.

standards. In the process, a new sprinkler and fire alarm network were installed, along with completely new electrical and mechanical systems. Access to the auditorium and dressing room levels for handicapped patrons was provided, with twenty-two wheelchair locations throughout the main floor. For the benefit of hearing impaired patrons, the Siemens/Sennheiser Infrared Listening System was installed.

With its improved sight lines and sound systems, the theatre can now accommodate the most sophisticated requirements of live theatre. There is no question that the Pantages Theatre is a far more comfortable and better equipped facility today than ever before. The result of the restructuring is that the theatre, not originally perfect for the presentation of drama, ballet, and opera is now equal or superior to many of North America's finest legitimate theatres.

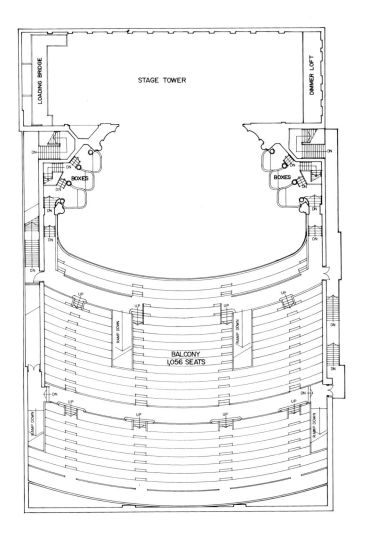

Floor plan of the balcony and mezzanine lobby.

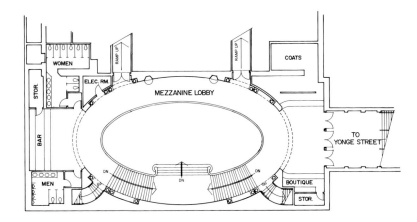

▲

When the Pantages was first built, the dressing rooms for the vaudeville performers were directly adjacent to the stage. In the construction of the restored theatre, the stage was enlarged and the dressing rooms were relocated beneath the auditorium floor. This photograph reveals the extensive excavation below the auditorium floor to accommodate dressing rooms for up to seventy performers. The concrete pillars seen in the centre of the photograph were constructed to support the new auditorium floor.

◄

The elaborate formwork for the new sloping auditorium floor can be seen above the excavated dressing room level.

▶

A view from the proscenium arch, looking to the rear of the auditorium. The structure overhead is the intermediate floor, which was constructed in 1972 when the theatre was divided into six small cinemas. This floor was used as a temporary platform during the elaborate restoration of the domed ceiling in 1989.

▶

The full domed ceiling is seen in one piece for the first time since the large theatre was divided into six smaller theatres in 1972.

A close-up view of a salvaged portion of the arch shown on the opposite page.

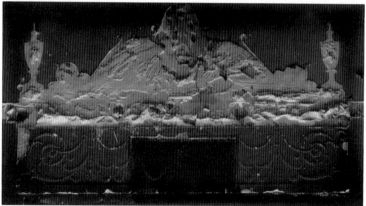

Plaster deterioration above the balcony emergency exit door.

The aesthetic aspect of the restoration problem was, in many ways, far more challenging to deal with than the functional aspect. Throughout the theatre's history, numerous alterations to the structure had seriously damaged or destroyed many of the decorative architectural details of Thomas Lamb's splendid original creation. The greatest damage by far was caused when the auditorium and stage area were split into six cinemas in 1972. The carved and gilded plasterwork of the proscenium arch was removed, the box seats on either side of the auditorium, with their decorative columns and plaster ornamentation, were destroyed, and the carved balcony fronts were obliterated.

A view of the private box seating, circa 1920, which was completely destroyed when the theatre was converted to six cinemas in 1972.

As well, intermediate floors and walls were constructed that split the great domed ceiling in half, destroying much of the remaining side wall ornamentation and decorative columns in the auditorium. Even the Yonge Street entranceway, with its domed ceiling, grand staircase, and delicate detailing, was painted over in bright red, black, and yellow colours. It's little wonder that the building that remained bore little resemblance to the glorious Adam and Empire-style movie palace that was Canada's premier showplace in 1920.

The existing condition and colour scheme of the Yonge Street link prior to its restoration.

◀
▶

The dome was severely damaged during the 1972 conversion to a six-cinema complex. Dividing walls were erected which cut through many portions of the dome's plasterwork. Those surfaces that remained exposed were completely repainted.

The process of paint removal from the grand staircase was extremely labour intensive, but the work paid off when the original finish appeared. It was fresh in appearance and deemed worthy of the restoration efforts that would be required to bring it back to its original lustre.

Craftsmen and artisans begin the laborious process of restoring the upper lobby.

Because of his well-deserved reputation, Dr. Hal Kalman, of Commonwealth Historic Resources Management in Ottawa, was retained to direct the restoration. Exhaustive investigations and analyses were conducted of all of the theatre's original finishes, colours, and fabrics, and studies were made as to how these might be duplicated faithfully in the restoration. Approximately 1,500 paint samples were taken from the interior surfaces and analyzed to discover the original colours and to ensure completeness of the colour palette.

Since the space was now almost completely reconfigured, care was taken to detail and to decorate all of the new areas in the style and character of the original, so that the new and the old would blend imperceptibly and harmoniously. Many of the original details and effects were re-created in modern materials, both to make construction easier and to conform to current fire safety standards. The old rayon and cotton jacquard-weave wall fabric was duplicated in fire-retardant modern fibres with the original colours and to the original design. Plaster ornamentation was prefabricated and installed in large sections inside the building. Steel framing was substituted for wood. In many instances, including the grand staircase railing, the scagliola (in which marble dust and different pigments are mixed into wet plaster) finish was exposed and restored, with new handpainted detail filling in areas where the finish had been destroyed or damaged. Many other "faux" finishes and effects were handpainted to duplicate the originals.

Elaborate detailing and effects have been used throughout history to give the illusion of grandeur. Some of the most commonly used

Multiple layers of paint, which covered the delicate scagliola finish on a stairway, are scraped away, revealing an artform rarely used today. Scagliola is a "faux" marble finish that appears throughout the Pantages' lobby and entrance. This marbleizing is achieved by mixing marble dust and pigments directly into wet plaster moulds. Originating in Italy, this technique is seldom seen in contemporary design because of the lack of skilled craftspeople. In areas where the scagliola was destroyed, painstaking brushwork was required to match the original marbleized finish.

A worker prepares the surface of an elaborate plaster moulding for gold leaf finishing.

faux finishes in theatres were scagliola and other painted effects such as porphyry, Caen stone, and false wood graining. Gilding, whether precious-metal leaf or imitation leaf, has traditionally been used to give the illusion that an object or detail was actually carved or cast out of solid precious metal.

The firm of David Hannivan and Company of Toronto, in association with other contractors, reproduced the special finishes and gilded surfaces of the original theatre by first repairing and patching broken plasterwork and then applying new finishes by hand. Throughout the lobby, extensive use of Caen stone walls and scagliola are examples of the theatre's many trompe l'oeil effects. In the oval lobby on the ground floor, the porphyry finish of the original deep blue columns has been re-created. The entire ceiling dome of this room is gilded in gold leaf. Some 75,000 six-inch-square sheets of gold leaf were applied and handcoloured, involving nearly 10,000 man hours of labour. Scagliola and marbleized effects were used throughout the theatre. Ironically, it is far more costly today to duplicate handpainted finishes than to use real marble because of the many hours of skilled labour required.

▶
Working from a scaffold, a painter applies colours that are identical to those that covered the ceiling in 1920.

Because the craftsmen working on the restoration needed accurate reference material, extensive drawings and photographs were made of every ornamental surface that remained. These documents thoroughly annotated all repair work and the finishes, techniques, and colours that were to be used.

Gold and silver leaf were applied throughout the Yonge Street entrance and lobby areas. Local craftsmen spent seven months on scaffolding in order to re-create the original delicate plaster motifs.

The Yonge Street link contains four identical vaulted bays, like the one shown here. The original colours and plaster mouldings were re-created from early photographs and extensive paint analyses.

A detail of one of the vaulted-bay ceilings.

A detail of one of the panels on the side walls of the Yonge Street link.

On completion of the restoration, crystal chandeliers were hung in each of the vaulted bays in the Yonge Street entrance. Their design was based on photographs of the chandeliers that were first installed in 1920.

Toronto artist Tony Philip's painting is based on black and white photographs of the original 1920 mural above the grand staircase.

▶

This view of the grand staircase, opening to the lower lobby, reveals the recreation of the wall mural and the replacement of the original stained glass window.

The colour scheme for the Pantages reproduces faithfully the effect that patrons experienced in 1920. Some thirty different colours have been used, ranging from yellows and ochres, through deep blues and greens, accented with pink and brown tones, and highlighted by silver and gold leaf. The firm of Magil Painting and Decorating carefully detailed the infill and background to recapture the grandeur of the earlier era.

In the Yonge Street entrance, two original murals were discovered, partially destroyed, behind mirrored panels. These were removed and expertly restored by artist Srebrenka Bogovic-Zeskowski, and they now grace the walls in their original locations. Unfortunately, the original mural that once occupied the wall over the grand staircase had long since disappeared. Toronto artist Tony Philip was commissioned to create a new work of art for this location in the classical style of the original painting. True to the tradition of the old masters, Philip painted his mural directly on the wall, working on scaffolding in the lobby. A fourth mural, which occupied the curved wall above the proscenium arch in the auditorium, will be re-created when the special staging effects for *The Phantom of the Opera*, which require the front of the auditorium to be painted black, are removed following the show's run. Also postponed is the gilding of the proscenium arch itself, which will also be completed after *The Phantom of the Opera* has closed.

As discernible from early photographs, beneath the staircase mural, there had once been a backlit stained-glass arched window set into an elaborate painted and gilded frame, but this had unfortunately disappeared. Serendipitously, while she was driving along a Toronto residential street, Julia Strutt, the project's design coordinator, discovered the original stained-glass panel on display in a second-storey window of a private home. The owners enthusiastically agreed that the panel should be returned to its original setting, so now once again it serves as the focal point of the grand staircase.

Much of the decorative plasterwork in the theatre was sculpted and cast by master craftsman Jean-François Furieri, of Toronto's Iconoplast Designs Inc. What Furieri found most challenging was the task of re-creating the two arched three-panel plaster screens depicting nymphs, flowers, and urns located above the box seats on either side of the auditorium's proscenium arch. These screens were rebuilt and sculpted on the model of an original panel found on site which had been broken into hundreds of pieces. The centre section was fashioned from a silicone mould considered to be one of the largest in the world. In addition to these two sets of panels, more than 3,500 new plaster casts were manufactured for use in replacing missing or damaged ornamentation in the auditorium and the lobby.

When the reconstruction process began, virtually all of the original plaster ornamentation had been either destroyed or badly damaged. Here restoration begins on the grillework that once covered the pipes of the theatre's enormous pipe organ.

The centre section of the ornate plaster organ grille is shown being crafted in the studio. This section of plaster casting required one of the largest silicone moulds ever made. The design of the grille was replicated by local artisans from the original drawings of the architect, Thomas Lamb.

The completed and gilded plaster organ grilles installed over the upper boxes.

Gold and silver leaf have been applied
to these prefabricated plaster ceiling
medallions.

This fully restored classical niche in the
Yonge Street Link is characteristic of
the Adam detailing employed by
Thomas Lamb.

The restoration work begins on the
domed ceiling from scaffolding that
was erected throughout the entire
auditorium area.

A craftsman carefully sands and repairs individual pieces of decorative plasterwork to prepare the surface for the final gilding and colouring.

Craftsmen apply prefabricated plaster moulds to a ceiling.

▶
As the restoration work progresses, the original splendour of the dome emerges.

Gold-leafed griffins and gold- and
silver-leafed medallions surround the
massive dome.

The totally restored dome. Hundreds
of man-hours were involved in its
faithful restoration.

EXTERIOR IMPROVEMENTS

Dramatic changes and improvements were also made to the exterior of the theatre. On Yonge Street, the original facade was rebuilt, and a new stamped-zinc and pressed-steel canopy with hanging bevelled-glass pendants was added. This beautiful structure was installed and assembled by Bernie Snitman of Toronto's Steptoe and Wife Antiques Ltd. The canopy, cornice brackets, and gargoyles were made by W.F. Norman Corporation of Nevada, Missouri, using traditional methods and turn-of-the-century dies and machinery. This firm has been manufacturing many of North America's theatre marquees and metal detailing for more than a hundred years. The key-shaped Pantages sign, with its white running lights and bronze finish, is a replica of the original, which hung over Yonge Street for just a few short years from 1920 to 1930. On Victoria Street, in an effort to enhance the theatre's presence on the street and to recapture the ambience of that era, a richly detailed brick facade has been installed which runs the full length of the frontage. This facade completely conceals and encloses the fire exit stairs that were formerly exposed to view. A new canopy matching the one that was erected on Yonge Street, and lit by authentic Victorian gas lamps, provides a sheltered and illuminated walkway that is enlivened by display cases and poster frames.

Wednesday, September 20, 1989 was the occasion of two special events, the official opening of the restored Pantages theatre and the Canadian Premiere of *The Phantom of the Opera*.

Even before the opening night curtain rose on *The Phantom of the Opera*, patrons were treated to music in the Pantages' lobby.

A triumphant opening night is celebrated by these theatregoers.

Even before the opening night, almost one half million patrons had purchased tickets to *The Phantom of the Opera* in the magical setting of the restored theatre.

The excitement and intense dedication of the restoration's team of professionals have been immense. For many of them, the restoration provided a once-in-a-lifetime opportunity to employ their most creative skills. The magnificent edifice that now constitutes this old, yet brand new, theatre is truly a triumph of accomplishment for all who were involved in assisting this particular phoenix to rise from the ashes.

On July 5, 1989, the Architectural Conservancy, Toronto Region, presented its Award of Merit to Garth Drabinsky for the purchase and renewal of the Pantages Theatre and for restoring and returning to future generations a landmark that may not otherwise have been preserved. Theatre architect, David Mesbur, and project manager and engineer, Peter Kofman, were also honoured for their involvement and dedication in helping to bring this vision to life.

The theatre officially reopened once again to an eager public on September 20, 1989, with the Canadian premiere of *The Phantom of the Opera*, a gala benefit performance for Toronto's Mount Sinai Hospital.

Harold Prince, renowned director of *The Phantom of the Opera*, expressed his appreciation and awe: "I saw this theatre at a stage when it was little more than an empty shell, and I realized even then its enormous potential. In spite of its size, it has a feeling of intimacy rarely found in theatres of its genre, probably because of its exceptional width. I have directed *The Phantom of the Opera* in London's historic Her Majesty's Theatre, in New York's Majestic Theatre, and in Los Angeles' Ahmanson Theatre. I believe that the Toronto Pantages will be the best of all of these theatres."

The original stained-glass exit sign.

Opening night guests leave the Pantages — Toronto's landmark theatre, now reborn.

PHOTO CREDITS

B'hend & Kaufmann Archives, 33; Canapress Photo Service, 57, 58, 66; Cineplex Odeon Collection, 43; City of Toronto Archives, RG 8 57-175, 20 (bottom) SC 407-17, 36; Columbia University, Thomas Lamb Archives, 74; Linda Corbett, 11 (bottom), 107 (bottom); Viola Ellis, 44; Kathy Fallona, 27; Mike Filey Collection, 17, 18, 19, 20, 22 (bottom & top left), 24 (top left), 25, 26, 41, 47; Paul Forsyth, 60; The Jackson-Lewis Company, 16, 34, 37, 39, 40, 42, 85; Yousuf Karsh, 7; Kofman Engineering Services Limited, 75; Richard Lamparski, 29; John Lindsay, 22 (top right), 23, 30, 31; David K. Mesbur, Architect Ltd., 75 (top), 79, 80, 81; Metropolitan Toronto Library, History Department, 49, 50, 52, 59, 60, 61; Margaret Morrison, 63; Joe and Ken Radford, 55, 57; Fiona Spalding-Smith, 2, 11, 12 (top), 13, 14, 68, 70, 71, 72, 75 (bottom), 77, 78, 82, 83, 84, 86, 87, 88, 89, 90, 91, 92, 93, 94, 95, 96, 97, 98, 99, 100, 101, 102, 103, 104, 105, 106, 107 (top), 109, 110, 111; Toronto Star Syndicate, 49, 50, 52, 59, 60, 61.